Honest to Goodness

Discovering the *Truth* and *Beauty* of a Loving God

Furman Buchanan

#2695

ISBN: 978-0-88028-527-8

Forward Movement

inspire disciples. empower evangelists.

Honest to Goodness

Discovering the *Truth* and *Beauty* of a Loving God

Furman Buchanan

Forward Movement
Cincinnati, Ohio

In memory of
Furman & Rosanne Buchanan,
my steadfast and loving parents
who taught me the Christian faith
by living it so well.

Table of Contents

Dear mortal, here's what I expect from you.

Dear mortal, here's what you can expect from me.

Dear mortal, I have some questions for you.

Dear mortal, this is how you worship me.

The week when God's actions speak even more loudly than words.

Easter Sunday

Another Easter Story & Epilogue

Acknowledgments

I want to acknowledge the beautiful people of Christ Episcopal Church in Mt. Pleasant, South Carolina, for enabling me to "think out loud" with them about the truth and beauty of a loving God. I also wish to thank my editor, Richelle Thompson, for her gifts of reading carefully, thinking deeply, and collaborating faithfully.

Introduction

The ancient prophets, poets, and storytellers of the Old Testament give modern readers a wonderful gift—the *words of God.*

These writers offer stunning commentary from God in all sorts of situations—religious, military, political, and social. Across thousands of years, they share the thoughts of God, often indirectly but sometimes with direct quotation. God bless them. The world needs faithful people who boldly attempt to translate the truth and beauty of God's love.

This daily devotional explores selections from Holy Scripture, including some of the most profound, surprising, and even hilarious words attributed to God.[1] A defining feature of these quotations is how direct and honest they are.

Designed for Lent but applicable any time of the year, this devotional book is curated for those who want to discover more about the truth and beauty of a loving God. We

1 Some of the quotations are paraphrased to accentuate their directness. For example, in some quotations, God switches to the third-person voice to describe God's self as "the Lord." In these cases, I have preserved the first-person voice throughout the entire quotation so it is clear that God is saying "me." In some of the longer quotations, I have omitted portions to help accentuate the bluntness and overall context of the idea. These edits will be identified.

examine some of God's own words so we might better understand who we are, who God is, what God expects from us, and—likewise—what we can expect from God. We learn how God wants us to worship. And we take a shot at handling some of God's most piercing questions.

On Saturdays, we hear what Jesus has to say. We discover the one-ness of the Father's love, revealed in the beloved Son through the power of God's Holy Spirit. Thus, each week culminates with Christ, *the* Word, who fulfills all the other words we've heard from God. Finally, during Holy Week, we consider how Christ's actions speak even more loudly than words.

The common denominator in all these words and deeds is honesty. And listening to God's honesty leads us to experience God's goodness. In other words, as we discover more of the truth and beauty of a loving God, we—ourselves—can move *from* honest *to* goodness.

God wants us to think, speak, and act in response to how God thinks, speaks, and acts in history—the more honest and good, the better. In a world filled with deception, greed, and violence, people of faith are called to stand up and speak out for honesty and goodness.

The best way to begin thinking, speaking, and acting in this way is by praying our own honest response to what we have heard from God. Therefore, each day's devotional passage concludes with a simple prayer.

We normally conclude our prayers with the Hebrew word, "Amen." The word itself means truth. So, in the spirit of expressing a desire for our honesty to become enacted for goodness' sake, I've chosen to translate the familiar "Amen" using an action phrase—"So be it!"

By the time we arrive at Easter, I hope you will find not only God's voice speaking through the words of the Bible but also your own voice as you take your turn alongside ancient prophets, poets, and storytellers to speak the truth and spread the goodness of our loving God in our own day.

Dear mortal, this is who you are.

The Opening Days of Lent

Ash Wednesday

You are dust, and to dust you will return.

Genesis 3:19

In the first creation story, God speaks order into a dark, soupy cosmos. In the second story, God begins by silently playing in the dirt. The storyteller declares that "God formed *adam* (Hebrew for 'man') from the dust of *adamah* (Hebrew for 'the ground')."

Hebrew is not the only language that literally spells out our intimate connection to the earth. Latin-inspired English also reveals the dusty, common denominator of our being *hum*ble, *hum*an, *hum*us.

Straightaway, we are tempted to reach far beyond our earthiness. We look for a magical shortcut to godliness—fruit that will give us knowledge to be like God instead of simply being ourselves. This is our first trespass.

The first trespass leads immediately to our second trespass—blaming someone else. The dirt-man immediately blames the woman, and the woman immediately blames the serpent.

When the Lord responds to this disobedience and deceit, we get a stark reminder of who we are, where we are from, and where we are going to end up…as humble, human, humus. "You are dust," says the Lord, "and to dust you will return."

From the very beginning, God speaks with brutal honesty about our mortal nature. It may sound bleak, but we need to know this truth if we are to have any chance of embracing our humanity and all the goodness that God has in store for us.

A Prayer in Response

DEAR GOD, why did you pick dust of all things? It seems so limited. I want to think of myself more highly than that. I want other people to think more of me than that. How did you anticipate humans like me having such a fierce, lifelong struggle with humility?

I'm tempted by shortcuts to become more knowledgeable and powerful—like you. And I'm inclined to blame someone else when things fall apart.

Help me to accept my humanity and to be myself. Help me keep in touch with my dusty, humble beginning…and ending. *So be it!*

Be fruitful.

GENESIS 1:28

In the first creation story (Genesis 1:1—2:3), God creates the heavens and the earth and all that is therein. The climax of this creative process happens when God creates humankind—male and female—in God's own image. Humankind is blessed with this spectacular, divine image and these invitational words, "Be fruitful!"

The first story of creation unfolds like a flower, day by day. The storyteller describes God's daily assessment—it is good...*until* the final moment on the last day when God creates divinely inspired human partners. This is when God's assessment changes. God looks, and indeed, it is *very good*!

On the one hand, we need to be reminded that we are dust. On the other, we need to be reminded that we share the very breath—the inspiration—of God. So, we try to live lives that are *both* grounded *and* inspired at the same time. We do this so we can be fruitful, for that is God's idea of what we are supposed to be in the first place.

Being fruitful means much more than having an inordinate number of offspring. Fruitfulness means flourishing—physically, spiritually, mentally—in peaceful relationships with God, other people, and all of creation. It means becoming fully alive, delighting in this gift, and sharing it.

Irenaeus, a bishop in the second century, proclaimed, "The glory of God is humanity fully alive." Imagine God's delight when we finally realize, as artist Pablo Picasso did—that "the *meaning* of life is to discover your gift, and the *purpose* of life is to give it away." This is what it means to become fruitful and—as a result—to glorify God.

The simple, powerful message for humankind revealed in the two creation stories is that we are not created to take fruit that does not belong to us. Rather, we are created to bear fruit that can be shared.

A Prayer in Response

Breath of life, I wonder why you are willing to share your own creative image with me. I don't think I can live up to your image or become as fruitful as you want me to be. Did you anticipate humans like me having such a fierce, lifelong struggle with self-doubt?

After creating humankind, your assessment changes from good to very good. It seems so optimistic.

Please help me trust that your divine image is indelibly marked upon me. And help me accept your invitation to be fruitful and generous with this gift, for goodness' sake. *So be it!*

Friday

Where is your brother?

Genesis 4:9

The original sin of humankind is trying to replace God rather than living fruitfully in the image of God and in partnership with God. The second sin of humankind is fixing blame on someone or something else.

The third sin—jealousy—arises in the second generation. In Genesis 4, Cain nurtures a jealousy so vile that he murders his own brother. And then lies about it.

God knows the answer but still asks the question, "Where is your brother?"

Cain replies, "I do not know; am I my brother's keeper?"

God's judgment is silent but clear as can be. The answer is yes.

The first story of God's invitation to creative, fruitful goodness is followed by stories of destructive and violent evil.

We must always remember that true human nature is not just good, but it is very good. Yet, God-given freedom of human choice is so broad that we can choose to reject our true nature and God's image—in ourselves and others. We can try to replace God and one another with shortcuts, blame, jealousy, murder, lies, and other sins.

God's judgment is clear. You are better than this. I made you better than this.

A Prayer in Response

DEAR GOD, source of all freedom, I wonder why you gave us the liberty to reject you and one another. Sometimes, it is hard to live with this much freedom. Did you anticipate humans having such a fierce struggle with you and with one another?

After creating so much goodness, you allowed us the freedom to choose so much worse.

Please help me trust that you made me better than this. Help me use your gift of freedom to choose goodness and to reject shortcuts, blame, jealousy, violence, lies, and other sins. Help me live up to my true human nature and to your dreams of a fruitful, generous, and peaceful human family in which we gladly accept the sacred duty to be our brother's keeper. *So be it!*

Saturday

I am the vine, you are the branches. Those who abide in me and I in them bear much fruit...

JOHN 15:5

Jesus has a lot to say at his last supper with the twelve disciples—reminders, directions, promises, and prayers (John, chapters 13-17). One powerful metaphor he uses is the organic, life-sharing connection between a vine and its branches. The vine is the ultimate source of nourishment and support for the branches, but it is the branches that carry the weight of fruitfulness and expectation of blossoming.

After Jesus invites his disciples to abide in his love the very same way branches abide in their vine, he re-states the new commandment he issued earlier that evening. "Love one another as I have loved you."

In that moment, a subtle and miraculous thing happens. Jesus promotes them (and us) from servants to friends. Are we ready for that kind of promotion? Are we prepared for

Jesus to have that much confidence in our ability to follow through with love as friends? Maybe not.

So, Jesus reassures us with a simple, profound reminder. "You did not choose me. I chose you." The branch does not choose its vine; it is the vine that chooses to send forth branches.

The good news in Jesus's assurance is that we have been chosen, nourished, and strengthened to bear fruit that will last. We are invited to become supple branches of a living vine whose fruit is the sort of loving-kindness one would naturally expect to see among good friends.

Notice how this vine and these branches bear forth the divine purpose that was first established with Adam and Eve. God's purpose from the very beginning has been fruitfulness.

Jesus's metaphor of the vine and branches helps us remember that nothing in all of creation is as fruitful as love. It is beautiful to behold, and it tastes as sweet as a well-ripened friendship.

A Prayer in Response

Loving Jesus, you sustain us with nourishment and strength for life. Thank you for choosing me to be your friend and trusting me to blossom, grow, and bear the weight of fruit that lasts.

I am taking you at your word. I will abide in your love. I will expect it to appear abundantly through me and in all the other healthy branches around me. *So be it!*

The HONEST Truth

We are created to be...

Humble

Fully Inspired

Keepers of Our Brothers & Sisters

Fruitful

For GOODNESS' Sake

Dear mortal, this is who I am.

The First Week of Lent

Sunday

I am God Almighty.

GENESIS 17:1

The transformation of Abram to Abraham is one of the most pivotal stories of the Old Testament. When Abram was ninety-nine years old, he was invited on a new adventure. The Lord appeared to him and said, "I am God Almighty [*El Shaddai*]; walk before me and be blameless."

This name, appearing for the first time in the Bible, can be translated as "God, the One of the mountains," but the main point it conveys is power. *El Shaddai* is capable of anything, including the miracle of bringing offspring as numerous as the stars to an old man who is as good as dead.

Here it is again—God's vision of fruitful abundance spread and shared throughout the earth for the blessing of the whole human family. *El Shaddai* even makes a promise for Ishmael, Abram's first son conceived with his slave-girl, Hagar: "I will bless him and make him fruitful and exceedingly numerous" (Genesis 17:20).

El Shaddai changes Abram's name to Abraham and immediately proposes to formalize their partnership in an everlasting covenant (*Berit Olam*). If the entire Old Testament had to be distilled down to two words, *Berit Olam* might be the best description of all. In fact, the entirety of our sacred story in both testaments of Holy Scripture is about God's desire to be a covenant partner with humankind for life.

A covenant is much more than a contract. Whereas a contract defines limits on how precise things of value are exchanged for a specified time, a covenant expresses a limitless, open commitment. God's covenant promise is both simple and broad: "I will establish my covenant between me and you… an everlasting covenant, to be God to you and to your offspring after you" (Genesis 17:7).

Just like dusty, old Abraham, we need the help of an almighty, powerful partner in order to become the people we are called to be. We need the strength of *El Shaddai* to do what we are called to do. The good news is that God has promised to give us this power and strength as an everlasting blessing. God is in it with us for life—everlasting life.

A Prayer in Response

ALMIGHTY AND EVERLASTING GOD, you have offered to partner with us for life. Embolden me to believe in your promise and trust in your everlasting covenant, especially when it seems impossible. Just as you transformed dusty, old Abraham into the father of many nations, you have the almighty power to help me change as well. *So be it!*

Monday

I AM who I AM.

Exodus 3:14

In the very beginning, God is described as *Elohim*, which usually means *the* God (above all others). Then, when Abram's name changes, so does God's—to *El Shaddai*, God Almighty. Abraham and his descendants keep the everlasting covenant with Almighty God for generations until the day Moses is called to become a partner. Moses has doubts—plenty of doubts.

"When I say to the Israelites, 'the God of your ancestors has sent me to you,' and they ask, 'What is his name?' what shall I say to them?" Moses asks.

God says, "I AM who I AM. Tell the Israelites that I AM has sent me to you." At that moment, near a burning bush on Mount Horeb, God claims another new name. It is not a noun; it is a verb! God claims the first-person form of the verb "to be." I AM conveys much more than "the God of our ancestors," a deity who acted in the past. I AM is a God who is acting in the present and who will act in the future.

We should notice the very first act of I AM because it is yet another pivotal story from the Old Testament. I AM overthrows oppression and slavery. I AM rescues the poor and abused. I AM demands liberty and justice for all.

This new name, spelled YHWH, is also unpronounceable—it has no vowels. It's just as well because the Israelites developed such reverence for their liberating God that they chose not to speak this name aloud. They used substitute words such as *Adonai*, "LORD."

Whatever name we may choose for God, it is helpful to think of God with a verb—not just as a deity who acted in the past with our ancestors but also one who is acting in the present and who is boundlessly free to act in our future.

Our prayers can remind us of this. In formal worship, we often conclude prayers with a doxology that proclaims the glory of God—Father, Son, and Holy Spirit—as it *was* in the beginning, *is now*, and ever *will be*, world without end.

A Prayer in Response

ALMIGHTY AND EVERLASTING GOD, you invited Moses to experience you in a new and personal way as one who acts in the present for the sake of freedom and justice. Help me to have more reverence for your holy name and for your action in the world.

Give me a thankful heart when I see your action in the past. Give me a courageous will to pray for your action in the present. Give me a hopeful spirit to dream of your action in the future.

O Lord, God of our ancestors and Lord of this present age and all that is to come, I praise your holy name. As it was in the beginning, is now, and ever will be, world without end. *So be it.*

Tuesday

I am the Lord your God,
who brought you out of the land of Egypt,
out of the house of slavery.

Exodus 20:2

I AM fulfills the promise to Moses and the Israelite slaves. They are brought safely out of Egypt (Exodus 14), and Moses sings a song about it (Exodus 15). This sounds like great news, but immediately the people begin to complain. They are afraid they will starve in the wilderness.

Several months into this tenuous experiment with freedom, Moses and his people arrive at Mount Sinai. Life in the desert has not been easy. The Children of Israel need guidance on how to live with freedom, justice, and peace… in other words, how to live abundantly with God and one another, even in the scarcest environment. This is when God once again speaks with directness and honesty.

"I AM the Lord your God, who brought you out of the land of Egypt, out of the house of slavery; you shall have no other gods before me."

An important thing to notice about God is the pattern of "give and take" that defines how the Lord relates to people. In this instance, God first rescues the people from slavery and then expects righteousness in return. Both the gift *and* the human response are intended to be for goodness' sake.

This pattern also appears in the other stories we have explored. God first blesses Adam and Eve with the Garden of Eden and then expects obedience. God first blesses Abraham with the promise of many offspring and then expects him and his descendants to keep the everlasting covenant.

In the Old Testament, we are getting to know God—the One who goes by different names but follows a consistent pattern. We are meeting the One who acts first and then expects a human response.

The expectations presented alongside these various divine gifts are just as relevant to us today. What shall we do with the gift of this abundant creation? How might we honor the everlasting covenant? How shall we follow the Lord's guidance for living with freedom, justice, and peace?

A Prayer in Response

DEAR GOD, I am beginning to recognize you by the way you act first and then expect a faithful response. Thank you for your gifts and blessings—creation, an everlasting covenant, and deliverance from slavery. Give me the courage to respond to your actions with good actions of my own. Give me the wisdom to trust your guidance on how to live with freedom, justice, and peace. Give me the boldness to take your gifts and then use them for your glory. *So be it!*

Wednesday

I am the Lord, that is my name.

Isaiah 42:8

Hundreds of years after Moses, during the days of the prophet Elijah, many Israelites abandon their covenant with the Lord. They choose instead to worship Ba'al, the god of the Canaanites. What a terrible trade.

In the Old Testament scriptures, we encounter the Lord, the God of Israel, as the creator, as a covenant partner, and as an emancipator. God does all of this for goodness' sake. And those who worship the Lord are invited to be fruitful partners in a divine mission of freedom, justice, and peace.

In those same scriptures, we also meet the Canaanite god, Ba'al, whose identity is like that of an impetuous, demanding landlord, dominating the people as if they are helpless tenants. So, we can see what a major step backward it is for the Israelites to stop adoring their freedom, justice, and peace-loving God because of their misplaced fear of a fickle, thunderous, landlord god. Really?!

Throughout the Old Testament, we have explored the calls of Adam and Eve, Abraham, and Moses. Now, in Isaiah (chapter 42), we hear a lovely song from God about the call of a servant. That servant is the entire nation of Israel.

This song describes the beauty of the Lord's creative power as well as the Lord's passion for justice and freedom throughout the world. This song expresses how God's own soul delights when his servant helps fulfill and spread the light of this peaceful vision among all nations.

This song reminds those people—and now us—that we are called to much more than fear of an impetuous, small-scale landlord god whose main tools of abuse and control are lightning and thunder. Instead, we get to worship and serve a God whose mission of justice, freedom, and peace is intended for all the earth. And we are reminded of the identity of this one, true God with a simple, straightforward proclamation, "I am the LORD, that is my name."

A Prayer in Response

DEAR LORD, creator of all that is, keeper of the everlasting covenant, lover of freedom and justice for all people; you alone are my God. You are like no other.

Not only will I worship and adore who you are, but I also will try to become who you want me to be—"a servant in whom your soul delights."

I want to help bring forth your justice. I want to help fulfill your peaceful vision. I want to magnify your light among all people for the glory of your name. *So be it!*

I call you by your name. I surname you, though you do not know me.

ISAIAH 45:4

An interesting development occurs three chapters later in the book of Isaiah. After we hear the Lord singing the first servant song about his chosen people, we get to see our God reaching far beyond Israel to call a gentile into partnership and anoint him with authority for a special mission.

This gentile is Cyrus the Great, King of Persia. His mission is rescuing the Israelites. Cyrus is called to set God's children free from a long exile in Babylon and help them rebuild Jerusalem and the temple.

As usual, when it comes to calling upon human partners, the Lord promises to do marvelous things for Cyrus with an expectation that Cyrus will—in turn—do marvelous things as the shepherd anointed to deliver and restore the chosen people.

Part of the fascinating nature of this partnership is that Cyrus does not know the Lord at all. Cyrus is not a Jew and never becomes a Jew. He is simply God's chosen, anointed, and beloved servant.

The prophet Isaiah helps show us that our understanding of God is too limited. We may think we know the Lord by name, but it is even more true that the Lord knows the whole, human family by name and calls them—whether they know our God or not.

A Prayer in Response

O LORD, you call us by name even when we do not know who you are. Give me the courage to answer your call when I do not have all the answers. I pray also for the humility to recognize that you reach beyond your faithful people in order to call strangers to your service.

I'm afraid my understanding of you is too small. Help me trust your understanding of me and the whole human family: you know us by name and call us by name. *So be it!*

Friday

A God merciful and gracious, slow to anger, and abounding in steadfast love and faithfulness...

Exodus 34:6

In the book of Exodus, we hear the thirteen attributes of the Lord as the Lord sees it. There are many other places throughout Holy Scripture where portions of these attributes are remembered. They form the best, most comprehensive summary of who God is.

"(I am) the Lord, the Lord, a God merciful and gracious, slow to anger, and abounding in steadfast love and faithfulness, keeping steadfast love for the thousandth generation, forgiving iniquity and transgression and sin..."

The Hebrew words in this speech make it clear that God is merciful 100 percent of the time—to those about to sin, those who are in the midst of sin, and those who have sinned. The Lord clears all sinners who sincerely ask forgiveness. God acts *for justice* but also *with mercy*.

So many things are ascribed to the Lord's doing by the prophets, poets, and historians of the Old Testament that we may feel queasy reading about it. Indeed, everything that happens is attributed to God—not only the good things but also bad things…even evil things.

These ancient writers did not think in terms of natural disasters. They interpreted natural calamities as punishing acts of God. (Incidentally, Jesus did not see it this way in Luke 13:1-5.) Neither did the ancient writers attribute manmade disasters to the men who caused them. They saw God hardening the hearts of oppressors and manipulating Israel's enemies to punish fellow countrymen for sins.

It is easy to see how nineteenth-century preachers like Jonathan Edwards manipulated Old Testament stories to make everyone feel as if they were just "miserable sinners in the hands of an angry God." This unfortunate view persists among angry preachers and fearful people today.

What if we instead trust God's own words about mercy, grace, and anger? What if we simply choose to accept the Lord's clear promise of steadfast love to the thousandth generation—not of the righteous but of miserable sinners who ask for forgiveness and a chance to start over?

A Prayer in Response

Dear Lord, my mind wants an explanation for why bad things happen. It is easiest to blame you, the one with the most power.

Help me accept that natural disasters are better explained with physics, chemistry, and biology. Help me see that human disasters are actually caused by humans who misuse their freedom in order to choose evil instead of goodness. Most of all, help me trust that while you may not act *upon* all things, you do act *through* all things just as you promised—with mercy, grace, and love to the thousandth generation. *So be it!*

Saturday

I am the way, the truth, and the life.

John 14:6

Throughout this first, full week of Lent, we have been introduced to God, who has been known by many names across more than a thousand years and along circuitous routes extending more than a thousand miles. This is not some petty, vindictive "landlord god" over one region or tribe or nation. From the beginning, our God has been inconceivably expansive, calling Abraham to become the father of many nations in order to bless the whole world with fruitfulness.

All gods are known for displays of power, but our God is known—in essence—as a verb: I AM. We learn through the story of Moses about our God's commitment to freedom and justice for all. This leads to the most pivotal action of the Old Testament—the overthrow of oppression and slavery.

We learn how our God delights when humans join this liberating effort—not only his beloved people but also distant foreigners who do not even know our Lord by name.

Above all, we encounter our God's distinctive character, unique among all other gods: "I am merciful and gracious, slow to anger, and abounding in steadfast love and faithfulness..." The Old Testament gives us a well-developed picture of a loving Father who wants all of his children in the human family to be fruitful, free, just, and peaceful in their dealings.

In the New Testament, we meet Jesus, the only begotten Son of this God, who personifies all these values. Using the name spoken by God to Moses, Jesus says, "*I am* the way, the truth, and the life."

In Jesus, we clearly see the glorious character of the Father by observing the glorious character of the Son (John 1:14). Jesus's expansive, inclusive heart is open to everyone. He is willing to sacrifice everything—including his own life—to make God's love accessible for all people. Jesus's compassionate, everlasting love is literally the way, the truth, and the life of God.

John, the evangelist, is right. "No one has ever seen God. It is God the only Son, who is close to the Father's heart, who has made him known" (John 1:18).

A Prayer in Response

LIFE-GIVING JESUS, you have shown us grace upon grace. Thank you for "fleshing out" what the love, freedom, justice, and peacefulness of God look like in a real, live human being.

Your way is my concrete example. Your truth is my guiding light. Your life is my precious gift. All I need now is the courage to think, speak, and live more like you. *So be it!*

The Honest Truth

God Is...

An Everlasting Partner

Liberating

Action-oriented

Calling Everyone

A Lover of Freedom, Justice, & Peace

Merciful, Gracious, & Slow to Anger

Full of Steadfast Love & Faithfulness

For GOODNESS' Sake

Dear mortal, here's what I expect from you

The Second Week of Lent

Be still, and know that I am God!

Psalm 46:11

So, how do we hear the words of a God whose first language seems to be silence? I AM speaks to Moses from a burning bush, but I have not been blessed with such a clear, unmistakable, audible voice in the wilderness. I'm not even sure I would want to hear God's audible voice. What if the words were in the language of my enemy? What if the accent made me feel like a distant outsider?

The scariest people I have ever known are those who were most certain of their own rightness in doing God's bidding. This is the danger of supposedly audible God-speech. It can fuel arrogance, extremism, and violence. People are never so vicious as when they feel certain they are acting for God. Those who are cursed with a false sense of certainty will do anything...except walk humbly with God and with their neighbors.

The psalmist dreams of a world that is falling apart. The mountains are quaking and crumbling; the sea is raging. In the midst of the chaos, the psalmist poet imagines God to be very near—not only a distant creator from ages past but a present helper for the here and now. "The LORD of hosts is with us; the God of Jacob is our refuge." Not just was with us but is with us—here and now.

The psalmist tells the story of our peace-loving God who makes wars to cease throughout the world. Our Lord breaks the bows of the aggressors. Our Lord shatters the spears of the oppressors. Our Lord burns the shields of the vicious enemies who want to destroy us. Then the psalmist suddenly stops the song, and there is silence for us to listen to God.

What is it that God wants us to do in the midst of chaos? What is it that God asks us to do when we feel surrounded and overwhelmed? The calming answer is a loving reminder of God's words: "Be still, and know that I am God."

In the stillness, we can experience the good news that the Lord of all the heavenly hosts is also here—with us. In our stillness, we take comfort that the God of ancient Jacob is still our refuge, even now.

A Prayer in Response

LORD OF ALL THE HEAVENLY HOSTS, I want to believe you are also my refuge and strength, a very present helper in times of trouble. I am going to be quiet now and delight in your silence for at least a minute…

I'm going to sit still, calm and humble with all my uncertainties for at least another minute…

Thank you for the gift of being still. Thank you for the gift of quietly listening and trusting that you are near—and that you are God, and I am not. *So be it!*

Monday

Hear.

DEUTERONOMY 6:4

Shema Yisrael—Hear, O Israel:
The LORD is our God, the LORD is One.

The very first thing God wants his children to do is hear… listen up…pay attention!

Just before Moses enumerates the Ten Commandments to the newly freed people of Israel, he gives a prerequisite command that becomes the essential confession of Jewish faith throughout the ages—*Shema Yisrael.* This confession—this commandment—is just as essential for Christians.

God's people are told to keep these words close to their hearts. Tell them to your children. Talk about them at home and everywhere else. Recite them before you fall asleep at night and as soon as you wake up in the morning. Bind them to your hand. Wear them on your forehead. Write them on the doorposts of your house and on your gates (Deuteronomy 6:6-9). In other words, do whatever it takes so you will not forget the One and Only who has saved us time and again.

It makes sense. How could I possibly follow God if I do not first pay attention to God? Listening is always the essential, first act of obedience. In fact, the word obedience is derived from the Latin root, *audire*, which means listen.

Listening is a clear and powerful act of respect. And if you think about it, respect is what the Ten Commandments are all about. The first four commandments teach us how to respect God. The next six commandments show us how to respect other people. The ultimate result of our obedience to all ten commandments is that we show respect for our own souls and bodies as the precious gifts that they are.

A Prayer in Response

Dear God, your love is the source of my life, and you have saved me time and again. I want to listen and pay attention to you. I want to respect you.

Help me to hold your words close to my heart. To do this, I will share them with my family and friends. I will repeat them to myself day and night. I will wear them like clothes. I will write them as a sign on my doorway to the world. I will do whatever it takes for me to never forget you, my One and Only. *So be it!*

Tuesday

Be holy, for I am holy.

LEVITICUS 11:44

In the beginning, the Lord is the source of creation. With Abraham, the Lord is the source of blessing and fruitfulness. With Moses and Cyrus, the Lord is the source of deliverance from evil and salvation from oppression. We should not overlook another essential aspect of God's life for the chosen people. The Lord is also the source of their ethics.

Traditional Jewish teaching describes human morality in terms of divine attributes. Just as the Lord is gracious, the people are called to be gracious. Just as the Lord is merciful, the people are called to be merciful. Just as the Lord is holy, so are the Lord's people to be holy.

The Book of Leviticus includes the holiness code of laws. Most gentiles are not particularly interested in all the ways our Jewish forebears sought to imitate the holiness of God in worship and in life. No detail is too small to be overlooked.

It can all be traced back to the Lord's command—"Be holy, because I am holy."

There is a marvelous beauty about an all-powerful God who takes weak and fallible people seriously. "Be special, just as I am special." Implicit in God's command is the expectation that we can actually do this—*we can be this!*

Imagine the glorious creator of heaven and earth taking you seriously enough to say, "Be special— because I am special." We are able to do this, though not by pulling ourselves up by our bootstraps. We are only able to do this by virtue of our proximity to the source of all holiness. The way to shine with the radiance of God's holiness is to get close enough for the glory of God to envelop you.

Kedushah, a traditional Jewish prayer, recognizes and honors God's holiness. Christians have adapted and incorporated this into our prayer at the celebration of Holy Communion, adding in the fact that we recognize Jesus as part of our source of life, blessing, salvation, and holiness.

What if we added another line to our prayer? Maybe we should take seriously God's expectation that we also can be holy—not by personal charm or grit or cleverness but simply because we are able to draw close enough to our holy God in order to glow in the proximity of our Lord's radiance.

A Prayer in Response

HOLY, HOLY, HOLY LORD, God of power and might, heaven and earth are full of your glory. Hosanna in the highest!

Blessed is the One who comes in the name of the Lord, Jesus my Savior. Blessed are we while imitating your holiness, delighting in your will, and walking in your ways for the glory of your Name. Hosanna in the highest! *So be it!*

Do not be hard-hearted or tight-fisted.

DEUTERONOMY 15:7

Money is not the root of all evil. Love of one's money is the root of all evil.

The reason is simple: money is power. When we cling to our power exclusively for our own benefit, we reject the needs of those without power (or with less power). Few things seem to rile God's anger more than greediness that either exploits or neglects other people.

Our heavenly Father cannot stand seeing some children suffering while others are hoarding. Nothing is quite as abhorrent in the eyes of the Lord as seeing the strong cling to their power while the weak members of the beloved family suffer.

The best way to avoid selfishly clinging to power is to not be so tight-fisted with our money. Where do we think it came from, after all?

Hard work? I wonder where I received the gift of this body.

Intelligence? I wonder where I received the gift of this mind.

Perseverance? I wonder where I received this strength of mine.

The truth is that we have been gifted with minds to think and hearts to love and hands to serve. In other words, we have received gifts of power from God in order to become fruitful members of God's family and to share this abundance—particularly with the poor who have less power and fewer gifts.

So, the Lord commands us, through Moses, "Give liberally and ungrudgingly…Open wide your hand to the poor and needy…" (Deuteronomy 15:10-11).

A Prayer in Response

Loving Father in heaven, keep me mindful of your love for your whole human family and your desire for me to share my power and fruitfulness with others.

How did you know I would be so tight-fisted in the face of so much human need? Replace my love for money with more love for you and my suffering sisters and brothers.

I want to praise you as the source from whom all blessings flow. I know the truest praise is to open wide my hands to the poor with thanks-*giving.*

You have given sacrificially of your abundance, power, and even life itself for the needs of your beloved family. Help me to be gracious and merciful, as you are gracious and merciful. *So be it!*

Thursday

Do justice, love mercy, and walk humbly.[2]

MICAH 6:8

A small-town prophet named Micah tells a story of how his nation has lost its way. He imagines a large, outdoor courtroom spread across the Judean hill country with the mountains and hills listening to the complaint of the Lord and the defense put forth by the people.

The Lord asks, "What have I done to you? How have I wearied you? Answer me!" Before the Lord allows the nation to answer the complaint, the mountains and hills are reminded of what the Lord has already done for them. "I brought you up from Egypt. I redeemed you from slavery."

The case is clear. The defense moves immediately to try to settle the dispute. "Shall I bring burnt offerings, with premium calves a year old?" Silence. "Will the Lord be pleased with thousands of rams, with ten thousands of rivers of oil?" The people are raising the ante! More silence. "Shall

2 King James Version

I give my firstborn for my transgression?" Complete silence. It is clear that God's people are willing to give anything to take away the Lord's displeasure with them.

After the defense finally stops bargaining, God sets forth the basic formula for faithful living. Even though God's desire is reported in a concluding comment by the prophet, let us listen in the first-person voice for emphasis: "I have told you, O mortal, what is good (time and again). What do I require of you? (All I expect is for you) to do justice, love mercy, and walk humbly with me."

When we feel as though God may be angry with us, we are willing to do almost anything to resolve the issue. Like the ancient people of Israel, we wonder what kind of transaction we can make to settle the matter quickly. Our God shows incredible restraint, not wanting us to make some expensive sacrifice as compensation. The Lord is not interested in a *quid pro quo* relationship of scorekeeping.

The Lord desires nothing more than for us to do what is right—justice; to forgive as we have been forgiven—with mercy; and to remain humbly aware of God's near and loving presence on our journey. And the Lord wants us to do these three simple but difficult things for life.

A Prayer in Response

GOD OF JUSTICE AND MERCY, you have called me to walk before you in holiness and righteousness all my days. How can I ever do this on my own? I need you to strengthen me so I have the strength to stand up for justice. I need you to encourage me to kneel down with mercy. I need to remember that you are God, and I am not. Therefore, I will walk humbly with you in the hope that you are showing me the way of life and also the way home to you. *So be it!*

Friday

It is too light a thing
that you should be my servant…
I will make you as a light to the nations.[1]

ISAIAH 49:6

During the first week of Lent, we reflected upon who God is, and we found part of the picture from the first servant song in the prophecy of Isaiah (chapter 42). In this second week, as we reflect upon what God expects from us, we need to look at the second servant song from Isaiah.

Both songs explore the idea that the servant of the Lord will become a light to all nations. The prophet Isaiah once again proclaims God's purpose to be the universal salvation of the entire human family. Israel is chosen as the servant who will illuminate this marvelous truth for everyone throughout the world to see.

God challenges God's people to do more than just serve their Lord. God actually wants them—and us—to serve the world. In our English, this makes a really nice wordplay:

1 English Standard Version

God says it is too light(weight) a thing to *just* be God's servant...and so God gives us as a light(source) to the world.

God dreams of God's people showing the world how to live with resilience. God believes that real, faithful people have a unique opportunity to illuminate for other people how lives and communities can be rebuilt and restored with freedom, justice, and peace by letting the light of God's steadfast love shine through them.

In the middle of the twentieth century, the Jewish people were cast down yet again. God's chosen people were subjected to the absolute darkness of ferocious, relentless evil in Nazi Germany.

Dr. Victor Frankl was a Jewish psychiatrist who survived two concentration camps during the Holocaust. Soon after his liberation, he wrote *Man's Search for Meaning* in just nine days. This book became an international bestseller. Perhaps it was too light a thing for Victor Frankl to just be a faithful servant of the Lord. Indeed, he became a light to a world in search of meaning. Indeed, he was a twentieth-century personification of the second servant song of Isaiah.

It is not easy to be a light. Frankl himself famously commented: "That which is to give light must endure burning." Nevertheless, God calls faithful servants to be lights in a world so often shrouded in darkness. God's eternal desire for the human family to share a common, meaningful life of freedom, justice, peace, and fruitfulness is always illuminated through real people like you and me. God knows we are able to shine with honesty and reveal the pathway to goodness.

A Prayer in Response

Dear God, you are the source of light and life. It does not feel easy being your servant. But then I read in scripture that you also want me to be a light to the world. I feel burned out just completing the tasks of each day.

God, give me strength to trust that your light is bright enough to shine through me. Help me remain open to you and other people. Maybe the cracks of my brokenness will enable the light of your hope and promise to shine through. *So be it!*

Saturday

I give you a new commandment, that you love one another. Just as I have loved you.

JOHN 13:34

At their last supper, Jesus shows how much he loves his disciples, loving them to the end. His miraculous love fully embraces his betrayer, his denier, and the rest of the disciples who are about to desert him. In other words, Jesus loves all of them—every last one of his disappointing followers.

In other teachings, Jesus has already explained that there is not only one great commandment (to love God with all of one's heart, soul, and mind). In fact, there are two great commandments, and the second one is just like the first: "You shall love your neighbor as (much as you love) yourself." All the Jewish Law and prophets are summarized in these two commandments (Matthew 22:37-40).

Well, at the Last Supper, Jesus raises the stakes even higher for his disciples. Their duty is not only to love the Lord their God and to love their neighbors but also to do so in the same manner and degree with which Jesus has loved them—unconditionally.

Followers of Jesus do not carry any sort of sign, bear a special mark, or wear designated clothing to show their affiliation. According to Jesus, the only way people will recognize his disciples is when they are seen loving other people as Jesus does. This is remarkably simple and incredibly challenging.

Our obedience to Jesus's new commandment is, in fact, the most simple and direct way we can fulfill all of the various expectations God sets forth throughout the Old Testament—listening, respecting, trusting, being holy, giving liberally, doing justice, loving mercy, walking humbly, and shining as a light to the world.

A Prayer in Response

DEAR JESUS, you have set a standard for loving that I can never fully attain. Nevertheless, this is the standard you have commanded for me. How did you know that I needed this ambitious challenge in order to remain focused on following you? Thank you for showing me how to be recognized as one of your disciples. *So be it!*

The Honest Truth

God Expects Us to...

Be Still

Listen

Practice Holiness

Be Generous

Do Justice, Love Mercy,
& Walk Humbly

Let God's Light Shine Through Us

Be Full of Steadfast Love & Faithfulness

For GOODNESS' Sake

Dear mortal, here's what you can expect from me

The Third Week of Lent

Sunday

I put…a ring on your nose.

EZEKIEL 16:11-12

Who knew? God gave Jerusalem a nose ring! Actually, as you might imagine, there is much more to this story, which is told by the prophet throughout chapter 16 in the book of Ezekiel.

It helps to remember that Jerusalem was initially a Canaanite city until the Israelites invaded in the thirteenth century BCE. It also helps to remember one of the tragic realities of ancient, pagan Palestine: female babies were considered a financial liability and regularly abandoned by their parents to die.

According to Ezekiel, this was the story of the ancient city of Jerusalem—she was abandoned and left to die. So, the Lord rescued her and made sure she would grow up to become like a beautiful woman. (Years later), the Lord said, "I passed by you again and looked on you; you were at the age for love…I covered your nakedness." Oh, dear! The plot thickens.

The crux of this part of Ezekiel's story is this: the Lord treated Jerusalem like a queen. Thus says the Lord God: "I bathed you with water…I anointed you with oil…I clothed you with embroidered cloth and sandals of fine leather; I bound you in fine linen…I adorned you with ornaments: I put bracelets on your arms, a chain on your neck, a ring on your nose, earrings in your ears, and a beautiful crown upon your head…You grew exceedingly beautiful, fit to be a queen."

So, what can we reasonably expect from the Lord?

The testimony of Ezekiel and other writers of the Old Testament shows that God wants to do more than just rescue us. God wants to help us become utterly and beautifully transformed.

We also have been adopted by God as living members of a royal family. As the rescued and utterly transformed Saint Paul writes to the Romans (8:16-17), "We are children of God, and if children, then heirs, heirs of God and joint heirs with Christ."

There is a shocking twist in Ezekiel's story later in chapter 16. Although Jerusalem was transformed by God to be as lovely as a queen, "she" ended up acting like a whore. In other words, she trusted only in her own beauty and was not faithful to God. How is that possible? This gut-wrenching question remains just as relevant for us. How can I so easily forget God—the One who rescued me, adopted me, and utterly transformed me?

When we are tempted to trust in our own beauty (or intelligence or hard work or wealth or family connections), it is important to remember the One to whom we truly belong. We can reasonably expect that the Lord who adopted us will also beautifully transform us through the power of love.

A Prayer in Response

LORD GOD, king over heaven and earth, you have treated us like royalty. You have adopted us as your beloved children, blessed beyond measure to inherit your kingdom. Why do I so quickly forget you? Why is it so easy to begin trusting in my own specialness? Help me never to forget that I already belong to you…and I always will. *So be it!*

Monday

I have tattooed you on my hands.[1]

Isaiah 49:16

Remembering and forgetting are prominent themes throughout the Old Testament. God sets the rainbow in the clouds in order to remember the covenant with every living creature (Genesis 9:15). The fourth commandment of the Lord calls us to remember the sabbath day and keep it holy (Exodus 20:8). The psalmist sings a prayer of hope that God will not remember the sins of his youth, but that God will remember him in accord with God's love (Psalm 25:6).

Shortly after the Lord challenges his servant, Israel, to be a light to the world, God's people push back. They say, "My Lord has forsaken me, my Lord has forgotten me" (Isaiah 49:14).

Surprisingly, God chooses a feminine comparison to show how ridiculous it is to think our Lord could forget us. "Can a woman forget her nursing child, or show no compassion for the child of her womb?" Well, God admits, "even these

1 This translation is from The Living Bible. The NRSV reads: "I have inscribed you on the palms of my hands."

(mothers) may forget, but I will not forget you." Then, God offers further proof to those who still have doubts. "See, I have inscribed you on the palms of my hands…" or, as The Living Bible recalls, "I have tattooed you on my hands" (Isaiah 49:15-16).

All of this is part of a song that praises God for the much-anticipated restoration of Israel from exile. The Lord promises that the desolate nation will become crowded again; all the scattered children of Israel will be brought home, and their oppressors will be forced to bow down and lick the dust off their feet.

The promise that God's dispersed people will be re-*membered* in their land begins with the promise that they have not been forgotten. Even devastated people are able to sing with joy when they imagine the powerful hand of the Lord raised up against their oppressors, and right there—tattooed on the palm—is colorful proof that they will be remembered forever.

This promise is just as real for us today as it was for the children of Israel in the time of Isaiah. Our Lord does not—could not—forget us. We are permanently inscribed in the most tender flesh of our God.

A Prayer in Response

O LORD, like a nursing mother, you hold us close to your breast. Like a passionate lover, you have inscribed us onto your hands forever.

When I feel alone, help me remember this. When I feel as if I have been forgotten, help me remember this. Help me, O Lord, to trust that you have not, could not, and never will forget your own beloved children, including me. *So be it!*

Tuesday

Open your mouth wide and I will fill it.

Psalm 81:10

Hunger and insecurity about food are facts of life in a harsh environment. The people of Israel experience food insecurity the moment they are rescued from slavery in Egypt. The Lord delivers them through the Red Sea, and they arrive in the wilderness, hungry and afraid.

"We used to sit beside the large pots brimming with meaty stews and eating our fill of bread back in Egypt," the people complain to Moses. "You have brought us out here into this wilderness to kill us all with hunger" (Exodus 16:2-3).

This is when the Lord, who has rescued them from slavery, begins to rain down upon them bread from heaven. It is everywhere, like a fine, flaky frost upon the ground. "What is it?" the people ask. Their question becomes the distinctive name for the bread of angels—*manna*.

When the people try to hoard the manna for themselves, it spoils. So, they are challenged every morning to trust that God will provide their daily bread—enough food to be shared by everyone. We are also challenged to trust God's provision and to resist the temptation to hoard. Like the children of Israel, we are challenged to share our daily bread for the sake of all who hunger.

The psalmist felt inspired to write a song about this. The song is about loyalty to the one who has saved us and who provides for us day by day. The people of Israel probably sang this song each year at harvest time during the Feast of Tabernacles. Known as *Sukkot*, this feast is still celebrated by our Jewish sisters and brothers every autumn.

Is it reasonable to expect the Lord who rescued us to also provide for us...day by day? Jesus teaches us to pray for this very thing when we say, "give us today our daily bread."

And the psalmist has given us God's answer to our prayer: "Open wide your mouth, and I will fill it!"

A Prayer in Response

GOD OF ABUNDANCE, in the time of your peoples' great need, you rained down bread from heaven.

Help me to trust that you also provide for my daily needs. I want to trust your abundance by not hoarding all that I have received. I want to celebrate your abundance by sharing it with others. I want all people to be able to sing your praise with full stomachs and thankful hearts.

Together, we will rejoice in the fulfillment of your promise that if we open our mouths, you will fill us—day by day—with what we need. *So be it!*

Wednesday

I will comfort you like a mother.[4]

ISAIAH 66:13

At the time Isaiah's final oracle was written, Jerusalem was being restored from her destruction and desolation during the time of exile. The people were rediscovering their hope for a better future.

The Lord invites the people to rejoice that their beloved city is once again like a nursing mother to them. "You may nurse and be satisfied…you may drink deeply with delight from her glorious bosom…you shall nurse and be carried on her arm, and dandled on her knees" (Isaiah 66:11-12). God desires and expects the children of Israel to experience tender, loving care in their beloved city.

In the very next breath, the Lord makes the promise even more personal by assuming the same tender, loving, feminine persona. "As a mother comforts her child, so I will comfort you…"

4 NRSV reads, "As a mother comforts her child, so I will comfort you."

We easily remember the masculine images attributed to God, such as king, father, or shepherd. We are also pretty good at remembering inanimate things used to describe God, such as rock, light, and wind. Why are we so neglectful of the feminine attributes of which God also spoke?

God's character is regularly described in the Old Testament as "gracious and merciful, slow to anger, and of great kindness" (Psalm 103:8 and many other places). Of all the images we employ to think of God, the best one might just be the tender, loving care of a nursing mother. Is there a more pure, holy, and humble picture of love than this?

During the last week of his life on earth, Jesus also uses a feminine image to describe his love. "Oh how I longed to gather you like a hen…," he laments over Jerusalem.

Might we in these days long to be gathered and nurtured with the tenderness of a loving mother?

A Prayer in Response

TENDER, LOVING GOD, you comfort us like a mother comforts her children. You nourish us in order to help us grow and become strong. You delight in us the way a mother delights when dandling her precious child on her knees. You want nothing more than to gather us up under your wings to protect us and keep us all together.

Help me to remember and trust these feminine images that you choose to describe your love for me and the whole human family. *So be it!*

Thursday

I will pour out my spirit on all flesh.

Joel 2:28

The prophet Joel lives through a plague of swarming locusts and interprets the devastation as a punishment from God. Naturally, he calls upon his fellow citizens to lament their sins, offer sincere worship to the Lord, and change their ways.

We hear Joel's prophecy on Ash Wednesday (Joel 2:1-2, 12-17). He offers a reassuring promise that it is never too late for us to turn back toward the Lord with all our heart. He also reminds us of the classic Old Testament description of God's character—gracious and merciful, slow to anger, abounding in steadfast love, and relenting from punishment.

Joel proclaims that if the children of Israel would honor their covenant with God and do what is right, the Lord would bless their righteous living with fruitful abundance and peace. The people could expect joy and gladness to return to their everyday lives.

As if this were not enough, the Lord then adds another spectacular promise: "I will pour out my spirit on all flesh..." What amazing grace! God is willing to share God's own Holy Spirit with mortals. Not only that, but God does not discriminate as we mortals do.

God clearly states that sons *and* daughters are capable of becoming prophets. God boldly proclaims that the young as well as old are able to dream and envision an abundant, peaceful life with God and neighbor (*shalom*). Finally, promises the Lord, "Even on the male and female slaves...I will pour out my spirit."

The generosity of our Lord is always greater than we imagine. We try to put limits and conditions on who God is or what God is willing to do. Yet, according to Joel's prophesy, God refuses to be restrained by our small, discriminating minds. When God says, "I will pour out my spirit on all flesh," all really does mean all!

At Pentecost, Saint Peter quotes this prophecy from Joel (Acts 2:17-21) and stretches it out even wider to explicitly include gentiles—friend and foe alike—from countries north, east, south, and west of Jerusalem.

It is not just that God has low standards for who is eligible to receive a blessing. God has *no standards*! As Saint Peter proclaims in a later sermon, "God shows no partiality...in every nation anyone who reveres the Lord and does what is right is acceptable" (Acts 10:34-35).

In other words, all means all.

A Prayer in Response

LIFE-GIVING SPIRIT, pour out upon us the abundant grace of our God. Cleanse the thoughts of our hearts so that we may perfectly love you and worthily praise you. Help us trust your promise, including your belief that all means all. *So be it!*

Friday

Put me to the test... See if I will not open the windows of heaven for you and pour down for you an overflowing blessing.

MALACHI 3:10

During Jesus's temptation (Matthew 4:1-11), he is challenged to prove God's ability to rescue him by throwing himself down from the peak of the temple. Jesus quotes from the Old Testament when he says, "As it is written, do not put the Lord your God to the test." This is written in Deuteronomy (6:16), when Moses urges the people to keep the commandments and trust in the Lord.

Yet, it is also written in the Old Testament that we *should* put the Lord to the test. In fact, it is none other than God who speaks these words, according to the prophet Malachi, during a time when the people are holding back with their thank offerings, their thanks-*givings*.

God asks an exasperated question, followed by a complaint: "'Will anyone rob God?' Yet, you are robbing me! But you (have the nerve to) say, 'How are we robbing you?'"

We learned last week of God's irritation with people who are tight-fisted toward their neighbors. It turns out that God feels the same way when we are tight-fisted with our tithes and offerings.

So, the Lord throws down this challenge—not only to the children of Israel but also to all of us who claim to love the Lord our God. "Bring your full tithe…and thus put me to the test; see if I will not open the windows of heaven for you and pour down for you an overflowing blessing."

If faith were a poker game, this would be the decisive moment when God pushes in a mountain of chips and calls our bluff. Am I sincere about my thanksgivings or not? Am I fully praising God from whom all blessings flow or not?

"Return to me," says the Lord of the universe, "and I will return to you." This is hard to believe at times. It can be hard to trust enough to open our tight fists and bring forth our full tithes and offerings. God knows this about us, which is why—when it comes to money—God reverses the instructions Moses gives to the people by saying, "Go ahead, put me to the test and see."

A Prayer in Response

O God from whom all blessings flow, I want to praise you by opening my hands as well as my heart. It is hard to believe you would open the windows of heaven for me. I do not want to put you to the test because it will also test me, and I'm afraid I might fail. Nevertheless, help me to trust in your generosity, even if I still doubt my own. *So be it!*

Saturday

I am the good shepherd...
And I lay down my life for the sheep.

JOHN 10:14-15

The Gospel according to Saint John clearly presents Jesus as the sacrificial Lamb of God whose blood is the atoning sacrifice for the world. Yet, in the middle of John's Gospel, Jesus presents an image of himself—not as a sheep, but as a shepherd—a good shepherd who will do anything for his flock. We celebrate this metaphor every year on the fourth Sunday of Easter, Good Shepherd Sunday.

The little town of Bethlehem is surrounded by rolling hills where shepherds tend their flocks. Those sheep are made to lie down in green pastures and are led beside still waters. Given its proximity to the temple in Jerusalem, this is where many of the unblemished, sacrificial lambs are born and raised. Some of these shepherds are the very first eyewitnesses of Jesus's birth.

Whether we think of Jesus as the Lamb of God or the Good Shepherd, it is beautifully ironic to picture him as an infant, lying in a feeding trough in the middle of all that green pastureland near Bethlehem. One way or another, he was bound for the temple in Jerusalem.

Our Father in heaven is also depicted as a good shepherd, not only in the beloved and familiar twenty-third psalm but in other places as well. Psalm 80 begins, "Hear, O Shepherd of Israel, leading Joseph like a flock…" Like Father, like Son.

This week, we explored how our Father rescues and cares for us. We received an indelible image of our Lord's commitment to remember us forever. We learned of God's promise to give us our daily bread. We discovered how the steadfast love of our Father is also the tender comfort of our Mother. All this goodness is poured out as if the windows of heaven are overflowing with blessings.

These beautiful images are summed up in the life of our Good Shepherd—a precious, one-of-a-kind life he was willing to lay down for us sheep. The Son of God was willing to live and die as one of us. At the liturgy for burial, we commend our beloved to God with these words: "a sheep of your own fold, a lamb of your own flock, a sinner of your own redeeming." In spite of all the biblical images of a powerful, transcendent, king-like God, the image we long for at the time of death is the modest image of a Good Shepherd who receives us with merciful arms.

A Prayer in Response

BLESSED JESUS, you are my Good Shepherd. I believe you will do anything for me because you already have. Keep me close enough to hear your call and follow your lead. When I stray and become lost, I trust you to leave the ninety-nine good sheep for your tender mercy's sake. I am thankful to be a lamb of your own flock and to share the comfort of your protection with any who are entrusted to my care. *So be it!*

The Honest Truth

We can expect God to...

Remain Loyal & Treat Us Royally

Remember & Re-member Us

Sustain Us

Hold Us Close

Pour God's Own Holy Spirit Upon Us

Shower Us with Abundance

For GOODNESS' Sake

Dear mortal, I have some questions for you

The Fourth Week of Lent

Sunday

Who let the wild ass go free?

Job 39:5

The Book of Job does not explain why bad things happen to good people, but it does reveal a lot about faith. This deeply challenging and beautiful story is relevant for all of time. It is our quintessential story for grappling with the suffering we experience through no fault of our own.

Job is a good person. For thirty-seven chapters, he keeps asking the question we sometimes ask, "Why me, O Lord?" And his friends toss out all the easy answers about human suffering, the same kind of worthless answers we've all heard. God just takes it all in—silently, patiently.

Finally, in chapter 38, God cuts loose on Job, poor fellow. "Put on your pants like a man, and I will question *you* (for a change)," says the Lord! "Where were you when I laid the foundation of the earth? Tell me, if you have (so much) understanding!" (Job 38:3-4).

Many of us grew up thinking God could be scary, but we never read enough of the Old Testament to realize that God can also be sassy. Nobody in Holy Scripture offers sarcastic jibes quite like the Lord of heaven and earth.

God's two speeches go on for several chapters. They are relentless and also poetic diatribes, revealing so much of the beauty and mystery of creation. The question, "Who let the wild ass go free?" is just one of many questions God asks Job. They all boil down to two essential questions: "Where were you when I created this wondrous world? Who do you think you are to question me?"

So, does this mean we should not question the Lord about our sufferings? No.

The obvious wisdom of the Book of Job is that we will not encounter God with easy answers. Job meets God through honest questioning and very patient listening. He does not give up. In the end, Job shows us how to challenge God—and be challenged by God—when life seems unfair.

A Prayer in Response

O Lord, my Creator and my Redeemer, I know it was you who let the wild ass go free. I also know I was not there to see it. Thank you for your marvelous and mysterious creation. Thank you for my own marvelous and mysterious life.

I'm still going to question you when life seems unfair because you're the one who gave me the strength and integrity to stand up and question what is unfair. I've also learned from Job that this is the only way I will meet you. You will not be found among the easy answers.

In this life, I do not expect I'll ever fully understand you, so I will keep questioning and searching. I trust that when my body is destroyed, I will see you…my eyes will behold you—as a friend and not a stranger.* *So be it!*

* This sentence from Job 19:25-27 is an opening sentence in the burial liturgy, The Book of Common Prayer, p.491.

Monday

Is it right for you to be angry?

Jonah 4:4

The ancient philosopher Aristotle advanced the idea of an "Unmoved Mover" acting powerfully upon the universe without being affected by it. Some references in our Holy Scriptures align with this notion of an all-powerful God who is constant and unchangeable.

Yet, most of the evidence from the Old Testament seems to point to the fact that God *is* moved—frequently! God *does* change God's mind—often! Remember when Abraham pleads with God to spare the City of Sodom from destruction? (Genesis 18:20-33). In a matter of minutes, God changes God's mind six times! It seems like God is always giving people more chances than they really deserve.

Jonah is the most hilarious prophet in the Old Testament. He becomes furious when God decides not to punish the people Jonah loves to hate. Jonah holds up a mirror for all of us who know that our Lord is gracious, merciful, slow to anger, abounding in steadfast love, and ready to relent from punishing. We love these characteristics of God…until we see them extended to our enemies.

When it comes to people we don't like, our preference is for God to take a law and order approach. Like Jonah, we get angry when God gets soft on other peoples' crimes.

Although the large fish receives top billing in Jonah's story, the most interesting part of the plot is when God's prophet finally and reluctantly does what God asks him to do—he warns the people of Nineveh. To Jonah's great dismay, those bad people actually listen to his warnings and are spared.

"Damn them!" Jonah keeps thinking (and hoping). He decides he would rather die than see God's goodness come to his foes. So, the Lord asks Jonah, "Is it right for you to be angry?"

We need to let this question soak deeply into our own hearts! After all, Jesus taught us to pray for our Father to forgive us our trespasses (only as much) as we forgive those who trespass against us.

The Lord provides a bush to shade Jonah…perhaps to help him cool down a bit! When the bush withers, Jonah loses it again.

And God is moved to repeat the question we all need to remember: "Is it right for you to be angry…*about a bush*?" Jonah has the nerve to answer, "Yes!" At least he is earnest in his stubbornness. Well, this sets the stage for our Lord to drive home the point of divine mercy.

"You are concerned about the bush which you did not create or care for. Should I not be concerned about...more than 120,000 people...and their animals (whom I did create and whom I do care for)?"

A Prayer in Response

MERCIFUL LORD, sometimes I feel as if I'm right to be angry. There are some trespasses I cannot forgive on my own. Help me follow your example of being moved to change my mind, to forgive and to relent from punishing. I need you not only to forgive my trespasses but also to help me forgive those who trespass against me. *So be it!*

Tuesday

Can these bones live?

Ezekiel 37:3

On the first day of Lent, we heard the words of God in the beginning—"remember that you are dust, and to dust you will return" (Genesis 3:19). Today, we hear the words of God when the prophet, Ezekiel, is sent out to a desert valley filled with dried-up bones, ashes to ashes, dust to dust.

This stark image is a metaphor depicting all the people of Israel. The meaning is very clear—God's people are not just dead; they are dead and gone. There is no life and no hope in the parched landscape of exile, just dried-up bones, dust, and ashes.

The Lord asks Ezekiel a question with a painfully obvious answer. "Mortal, can these bones live?" Of course not. Except the prophet believes that nothing is too wonderful for God, and so Ezekiel replies, "You know the answer."

On the second day of Lent, we were reminded how the dust of the earth came alive when God breathed God's own Spirit into it (Genesis 2:7). It happened once; maybe it could happen again.

And then it does happen! Ezekiel, with a dramatic flair, describes how "suddenly there was a noise, a rattling, and the bones came together…there were sinews on them, and flesh…and the breath came into them, and they lived, and stood on their feet, a vast multitude" (Ezekiel 37:7-10).

The beauty of this dramatic story is its revelation that we not only return to the dust but also we return to the source of our life. God speaks through Ezekiel to assure us with this promise: "You will know who I am when I bring you up from your graves…I will put my spirit within you, and you will live" (Ezekiel 37:13, 14).

If we are to live honestly, we must remember that we are dust and that death is real. If we are to live hopefully, we should also remember that even our dusty, dry bones belong to God.

In the end, this prophetic story from Ezekiel reveals a hopeful twist on God's words from the very beginning of Genesis: "Remember that you are dust, and to *Me* you shall return."

A Prayer in Response

BREATHE ON ME, Breath of God,
fill me with life anew,
that I may love what thou dost love,
and do what thou wouldst do.

Breathe on me, Breath of God,
so shall I never die;
but live with thee
the perfect life of thine eternity.

So be it!

—Edwin Hatch
The Hymnal 1982, #508

Wednesday

Do I eat the flesh of bulls, or drink the blood of goats?

PSALM 50:13

We met the Lord in a courtroom during the second week of Lent when Micah described what God really wants from us—justice, mercy, and humility. In Psalm 50, the Lord reappears in a courtroom, this time with a lawsuit accusing us mortals of failing to keep up our end of the deal.

"I will take no bull from you," says the Lord. Although referring to sacrificial bull calves, I find a double meaning in this statement. God is obviously frustrated by the peoples' hypocrisy. They casually disregard their covenant with the Lord all week long and then arrive with sacrificial lambs… goats, bulls, and birds as if the animals will cover up the peoples' entrenched patterns of disobedience.

"Every wild animal of the forest is (already) mine; all the herds of cattle on the hillsides—mine; all the birds of the air—mine; every creature in the fields—mine!" says the

Lord. As if this rebuke is not clear enough, the Lord states plainly, "(Even) if I *were hungry*, I would not tell you!"

This leads to one of the most sarcastic questions in all of Holy Scripture: "Do you (actually) think I eat the flesh of bulls, or drink the blood of goats?" asks the Lord. The answer is obvious. No!

We must be careful not to ignore these rebukes regarding sacrificial worship practices despite the fact that they were never adopted by the Christian community. Indeed, the Jewish people ultimately moved beyond a theology of sacrificial atonement for sins in a way that most Christians could never dream of doing. Let's face it: we've become so enamored with the idea of Jesus as the lamb who takes away our sins that we can fail to see him as the pioneer of the faithful obedience we are called to practice each day.

Maybe we need to reimagine our own theology of sacrificial atonement for sins to ensure we are not devaluing the importance of daily, faithful obedience to God's ways (of justice, mercy, and humility). Maybe we need to remember what our Jewish ancestors learned and accepted 2,000 years ago—our Father in heaven is more interested in covenant faithfulness than in sacrificial blood.

A Prayer in Response

HEAVENLY FATHER, I know that you have no appetite for bull, and so I will be perfectly honest. It is easier to lean on your Son's sacrifice than to stand up straight and follow his example.

Please give me ears to hear your rebuke when I assume that my Sunday worship will easily take care of my Monday-through-Saturday neglect of your expectations. And then, give me the courage to change not only my assumptions but also my ways. *So be it!*

What are you doing here?

1 Kings 19:9,13

The great prophet Elijah served the Lord during the reign of King Ahab in the ninth century BCE. His central prophecy to the wayward king and the children of Israel is summed up in the literal meaning of his name, *El-i-Jah*—the Lord is God. (In other words, Ba'al is not.)

In the far north region of Sidon, a gentile widow with a dying son displays tremendous faith, and Elijah brings the child back to life (1 Kings 17:8-24). Then, at Mt. Carmel, within the northern kingdom of Israel, Elijah—the last remaining prophet of the Lord —is involved in an unforgettable contest against 450 prophets of Ba'al (1 Kings 18:20-40). Elijah is accustomed to experiencing (and revealing) the Lord, the God of Israel, in remarkably dramatic ways.

Despite the obvious truth of Elijah's prophesy, evil Queen Jezebel plans to kill him. So, Elijah runs for his life, fleeing to the southern kingdom of Judah. In fact, he keeps running farther south for forty days and hundreds of miles until he finally reaches Mt. Horeb (a.k.a. Mt. Sinai), where another mighty prophet, Moses, had ascended after fleeing from Egypt. The Lord asks Elijah, "What are you doing here?" This is a great question for all of us to ponder. What am I running from? What am I called to do—here and now? Elijah feels as if he is all alone, and there is no one else left to stand up and speak out for the Lord.

Suddenly, a terrifying wind swirls around Elijah, powerful enough to split rocks into pieces, but the Lord is not in the wind. Next, a mighty earthquake shakes the ground beneath the prophet's feet, but the Lord is not in the earthquake. Then, a raging fire erupts before his eyes, but the Lord is not in the fire.

Elijah expects to find God in the dramatic, just like we do. Instead, Elijah discovers God in the sound of sheer silence, just like we do. On a lonely mountaintop in a vast desert, God's last living prophet looks out from a cave. Silence is all he can hear, and it is enough. Elijah remains still and breathes in the silent, powerful, and promising Spirit of God. This is when the voice returns...with the very same question: "What are you doing here, Elijah?"

We can benefit by asking ourselves this same challenging question. What am I doing here? Am I willing to be still and listen to God in the silence? What am I ready to do, say, or give away for the glory of God—here and now—as if I was the last, living prophet around?

A Prayer in Response

LORD GOD, lover of silence, be near when I am afraid. Uphold me when I feel alone. Encourage me when I am terrified by great winds or earthquakes or fires or enemies. Help me to be still and trust your silent presence. Challenge me to think about why I am here. And then refresh me with strength for the rest of my journey until the last day when I return completely to you. *So be it!*

Friday

What do you mean
by crushing my people,
by grinding the face of the poor?

ISAIAH 3:15

We have already heard how the prophet Micah envisioned the children of Israel on trial in a courtroom with the Lord acting as prosecutor. Earlier this week, we experienced another courtroom scene from Psalm 50, with God as judge and the earth and heavens summoned as witnesses in a covenant "lawsuit" against God's people.

In this passage, Isaiah also envisions a courtroom drama, with the Lord acting as both prosecutor and judge. This time, the defendants are the elders and princes, members of the ruling class who have bent the rules to legally plunder the already scarce resources of the poor.

The Lord is furious at just how brazenly the wealthy and powerful leaders have exploited the poor and vulnerable who are their fellow citizens. "What do you mean by crushing my people?" asks the Lord. "(What do you mean) by grinding the face of the poor?"

There is no answer offered in response to the Lord's damning question because there is no defense for those who have the means to help the poor but choose instead to abuse them even more. In God's eyes, this behavior is defenseless.

It does not matter to God if our actions are—strictly speaking—legal because God knows how crafty we can be in tweaking the laws and economy to tilt the odds in our favor. When the Lord rises to argue the case against those who are wealthy and powerful, the only thing that matters to God is the suffering endured by God's other children, the ones who are poor and vulnerable.

Isaiah predicts the downfall of the rich and haughty who live in the upscale neighborhoods of Jerusalem—scabs on their heads, a stench in their streets, and the stripping away of their jewelry, fine robes, and linens. Instead of well-set hair, the women shall become bald. Instead of security, the men shall fall by the sword. Isaiah describes how the beauty of the rich will be replaced with shame (Isaiah 3:16-26).

The conclusion we can draw from this courtroom drama is that God relentlessly questions why some members of God's family are doing so well while others are suffering so terribly. And God is not interested in hearing what is "legal." God is only interested in what is just and merciful.

A Prayer in Response

LORD GOD, prosecutor and judge of those who crush the poor members of your human family, give me eyes to see justice the way that you see justice. Challenge me to resist taking comfort in what is legal but nevertheless grinds the face of the poor. Inspire me to stand up and speak out for laws and policies that help lift up the vulnerable and protect them from the greedy. *So be it!*

What is it you want me to do for you?

MARK 10:36, 51

Jesus is about to ascend the steep road from Jericho to Jerusalem for the final week of his earthly life. We get to hear a conversation he has with James and John, the two brothers who—years earlier—dropped their fishing nets immediately in order to follow Jesus. They sense that the time is right to ask for a special favor: "Teacher, we want you to do for us whatever we ask."

It is Jesus who asks the question, though. "What is it you want me to do for you?"

We can be thankful that we follow a Lord who is willing to listen to our needs and wants without prejudging us. It's one of the ways Jesus shows us how to respect the dignity of every human being.

Unfortunately, James and John do not ask for a very dignified favor. Rather, they just want to be the first disciples to claim the best V.I.P. seats imaginable.

Jesus responds with honesty, "You do not know what you are asking!" Jesus has taught them over and over that following him involves hardship, danger, suffering, and death. And he is smart enough to know that nobody really wants a "front-row seat" for any of that.

Predictably, the other ten disciples are angered by the Zebedee brothers' power play. And this affords Jesus an opportunity to restate his life's purpose: "The Son of Man came not to be served, but to serve." And Jesus longs for us to follow his example.

So, in the very next story, Jesus shows us how to serve. A destitute blind man is shouting from the roadside, and is being shushed. Jesus, however, wants to meet him. When the man approaches, Jesus asks this total stranger the very same question he just asked his two disciples: "What do you want me to do for you?"

We get to see Jesus once again operate without prejudice. We also get a lesson in praying for necessities rather than privileges, because the poor man simply says, "My teacher, let me see again!"

There is good news in these two stories that feature the same question. First, we can trust that Jesus really wants to hear what we need in order to live faithful and fruitful lives of service. And, second, he is willing to listen and respond to our petitions with honesty and goodness.

In the Book of Common Prayer, the collect featured for the Sunday closest to July 20 beautifully summarizes our dependence upon the mercy and worthiness of Jesus Christ to grant our desires and petitions as may be best for us and not necessarily as we ask.

A Prayer in Response

Almighty God, the fountain of all wisdom, you know our necessities before we ask and our ignorance in asking: Have compassion on our weakness, and mercifully give us those things which for our unworthiness we dare not, and for our blindness we cannot ask; through the worthiness of your Son Jesus Christ our Lord, who lives and reigns with you and the Holy Spirit, one God, now and forever. *So be it!*

—The Book of Common Prayer

The Honest Truth

God Wants Us to Be Clear That...

God is God, and We Are Not

Our Righteous Anger Is Not Impressive

We Should Dream Big & Hope Big

God Won't Take Our Bull, Just Our Mercy

We Can Trust in God's Calm Silence

We Better Not Crush the Poor

For GOODNESS' Sake

Dear mortal, this is how you worship me.

The Fifth Week of Lent

Sunday

Say to them,
"The Lord bless you and keep you..."

Numbers 6:23b-24

After the great escape from slavery in Egypt, the Lord helps Moses get organized. The book of Numbers begins with all sorts of peculiar laws and instructions for how the twelve tribes of Israel will live with God and one another. One of those twelve tribes—the Levites—is set aside for an essential purpose. Aaron (Moses's brother) and his descendants are called to be priests who facilitate the relationship between God and the people. Their job is to help everyone else reach out to God in worship.

The Lord instructs Moses to tell Aaron and his sons what they are supposed to tell the people. "Say this: 'The Lord bless you and keep you; the Lord make his face to shine upon you, and be gracious to you; the Lord lift up his countenance upon you, and give you peace.'"

The good news revealed through these words is that our God wants to bless us, not destroy us. As I mentioned on

Wednesday of the first week of Lent, the ancient peoples' imaginations were filled with dangerous, temperamental, and spiteful gods wreaking havoc in the heavens and upon the earth. Although our Old Testament contains plenty of notes of frightening encounters and even fierce punishments, the clear and dominant melody that resonates throughout the narrative and lingers in our hearts and minds describes a very different kind of God—one who blesses.

From the beginning, our God has blessed humankind with life, overflowing with blessings abundant enough to be shared. From the beginning, God's will is for humans to experience and share fruitfulness, generosity, freedom, justice, mercy, and peace.

So, when God's liberated people reach out through worship to reaffirm their desire to live in accordance with God's will (spelled out in God's law), the priests are supposed to pronounce the Lord's blessing clearly and poetically upon them.

We still want to believe that God is willing to bless us and keep us. We want to dream of God's benevolent face shining with approval upon us. We want to imagine our creator being steadfastly gracious to us. We want the assurance of our Redeemer's merciful countenance to give us peace.

All of this is promised to us through this ancient Jewish blessing that never gets old.

Unlike all those other ancient gods, our Lord is most passionate about one thing—blessing. Our God is just different. Our Lord has a face that shines with adoration for us. Our Lord has a merciful countenance and a peaceful spirit. We are fortunate to imagine God saying, "You are blessed. I love you. I want you to enjoy and share a fruitful, generous, free, just, merciful and peaceful life with me and with your neighbors."

A Prayer in Response

LORD, lift up your face and let me see your loving-kindness shining upon me. Lord, bless me and keep me within your gracious favor. Lord, strengthen my confidence in your blessing so that I will pronounce it and share it with my neighbors. *So be it!*

Monday

Rend your hearts
and not your clothing.

JOEL 2:13

The ancient Jewish custom of *Kriah* or tearing of clothes is an outward and visible sign of grief and mourning recorded throughout the Old Testament. Some Jewish family members still practice this symbolic act prior to a funeral for their beloved. Others wear a torn black ribbon.

Symbols and rituals serve as outward and visible signs that help direct our attention to inward and spiritual realities. Joel helps illuminate this connection with regard to the practice of *Kriah*, quoting the Lord, who says, "Tear apart your hearts, not (just) your clothes."

This speech—one of the possible Old Testament lessons for Ash Wednesday—calls for deep, heartrending sorrow about our transgressions. Simply put, if you worthily lament your sins, you will feel "torn up" about them.

Sincere regret about our trespasses motivates us to seek forgiveness and reconciliation with God and with our neighbors. Sincere regret about the righteous things we have left undone forges a stronger commitment within us to follow the Lord's example.

In the very next sentence, Joel reminds us what this example looks like: "Return to the LORD, your God," Joel urges, "who is gracious and merciful, slow to anger, and abounding in steadfast love, and relents from punishing." On Friday of the first full week of Lent, we learned of this classic description of God's character that appears throughout the Old Testament.[7] We are blessed to follow a God whose essence makes forgiveness not only possible but also desirable.

Psalm 51—also appointed for Ash Wednesday—is the quintessential expression of heartrending sorrow about our sinfulness. We pray, "Create in me a clean heart, O God, and put a new and right spirit within me." The most efficient way for God to perform this kind of healing and renewal is if we tear open our broken hearts and invite our great physician to work on them.

7 Here are some other places you will find the classic definition of God's character: Numbers 14:18, Nahum 1:3, Psalms 86:15, 103:8, 145:8, Nehemiah 9:17, and Jonah 4:2.

A Prayer in Response

ALL-FORGIVING GOD, I do not want to expose my torn-up heart, even though I believe you are gracious and merciful. I am afraid to be completely honest about my sins, even though I believe you are slow to anger. I am reluctant to submit myself to such deep, interior change, even though I believe you are abounding in steadfast love and will relent from punishing as I deserve.

I know in my heart that a broken heart does not need protection; it needs cleansing, healing, and restoration, as only you can give. So, "create in me a clean heart, O God, and put a new and right spirit within me!" *So be it!*

Tuesday

No one shall appear before me empty-handed.

Exodus 34:20

The Old Testament gives clear notice that God will not be bribed, nor is it possible for us to "pay off" the Lord for our sins with offerings that are purely transactional and devoid of intention to amend our lives and follow the ways of God. We reviewed classic examples of this with the prophet Micah on Thursday of the second week of Lent and again last Wednesday when we examined Psalm 50.

On the other hand, our Holy Scriptures give us equally clear notice that we should not appear before God empty-handed. Indeed, those who claim to be devoted to the Lord are expected to present the first fruits of our lives, not the leftover residuals after satisfying all of our other needs and desires.

God's expectation of first fruits is expressed in this passage from Exodus. The children of Israel are called to offer to the Lord all firstborn cows, sheep, donkeys, and sons (see also

Exodus 13:2, 12). In the case of donkeys and sons, there is a provision for them to be redeemed—"bought back"—with some other substitute offering.

The most familiar example of presenting and redeeming a firstborn son is found in the Gospel according to Luke (2:22-24). In this story, Jesus is presented to the Lord in the temple and then redeemed with a pair of turtle doves because Mary and Joseph could not afford a sacrificial lamb. (Leviticus 12:8 offers this special concession for parents who are poor.)

The reason God calls upon the children of Israel to present their first fruits is not only because the Lord is holy and worthy to be praised but also because the Lord considers the firstborn of the Israelites holy and worthy. It all goes back to that fateful night in Egypt when all the firstborns of the oppressors were struck down so the Israelites could escape from slavery. On that holy night, each Israelite family sacrificed a Passover Lamb in order to set apart their own firstborn to be saved, and God has considered them to be holy ever since (Numbers 8:17-18).

The most appropriate way to look at God's call to bring offerings is not that we have to do it, but that we get to do it! We offer our sacrifices of praise and thanksgiving because God considers us to be holy, set apart, and worthy to be saved.

Many of us who grew up attending worship remember singing, "Praise God from whom all blessings flow…" as the offering plates were brought forward. Some of us believe it. Fewer of us act upon that belief by praising God with the generous offering of our own first fruits.

A Prayer in Response

Eternal, life-giving God, I can believe that you are holy. Help me remember that you have made me holy as well.

You redeemed me through a very large sacrifice. So, I will not show up empty-handed when I praise you. I want to truly honor you as the source of all my blessings by offering at least some of my first fruits. *So be it!*

Wednesday

Even though you make many prayers,
I will not listen.

ISAIAH 1:15

Isaiah's prophecy begins with the Lord speaking an angry diatribe. As we learned last week from the sarcasm of Psalm 50, God's people thought they could simply appease the Lord's displeasure about their injustices. Wrong!

"I have had enough of burnt offerings of rams and the fat of fed beasts; I do not delight in the blood of bulls or of lambs or of goats…I cannot endure (your) solemn (worship) assemblies. Your…appointed festivals my soul hates; they have become a burden to me...When you stretch out your hands, I will hide my eyes from you…even though you say many prayers, I will not listen…" (Isaiah 1:11-15).

The Lord is furious about the people's hypocrisy. The Lord is sick and tired of those who ignore the needs of the poor, showing up to worship as if nothing is wrong. The Lord rejects one-day-a-week worship alongside six-days-a-week abuse and neglect of our vulnerable neighbors.

What does God want? In verses 16 and 17, the Lord names seven clear expectations for people who want their prayers to be heard and their worship to be appreciated:

1. Wash yourself, make yourself clean (from these evil things)
2. Cease doing (these) evil (things)
3. Learn to do good
4. Seek justice
5. Rescue the oppressed
6. Defend orphans
7. Plead for widows

Much later in Isaiah's prophecy (chapter 58), God expresses similar frustrations and preferences related to peoples' worship practices. "Is not *this* the worship I choose: to loose the bonds of injustice, to undo the thongs of the yoke, to let the oppressed go free, and to break every yoke (burden)? Is it not to share your bread with the hungry, and bring the homeless poor into your house; when you see the naked, to cover them, and not to hide yourself from your own kin (who are in need)?"

A Prayer in Response

LORD, HAVE MERCY. I am not worthy to praise your holy name. I have caused abuse, ignored injustice, and neglected human suffering. And yet, I know your character is always to have mercy, even upon those—like me—who have been merciless in the past. Please accept my sincere regret. I want to be better at giving you the kind of worship you choose—seven days a week. *So be it!*

Thursday

Let justice roll down like waters.

AMOS 5:24

In 750 BCE, many people thought Israel was doing great—it was a mostly peaceful time, and prosperity was rising. The religious leaders believed God was blessing the country with special favor. The people who felt blessed, personally, also felt quite comfortable with the societal order of things.

When we experience good fortune, it is easy to overlook those who are less fortunate. When we focus on how our hard work contributes to success, it becomes harder to see the people and systems that help make our successes possible.

The prophet, Amos, is not a religious professional, and neither was his father. Amos is a small-town guy, a simple shepherd, an uneducated pruner of sycamore trees. This unlikely prophet has the temerity to quote the Lord of heaven and earth. "I hate, I despise your (religious) festivals, and I take no delight in your solemn (worship) assemblies."

Just imagine if a rural lumberjack decided to confront your professionally trained clergy about liturgical matters?

Amos continues to speak the words of the Lord: "Take away from me the noise of your songs; I will not listen to the melody of your harps." Just imagine a goat herder from the country lecturing your church organist and choir members like this.

Comfortable, religious people seem perpetually at risk for overlooking the uncomfortable complaints of outsiders. This was true more than 2,700 years ago when an outsider named Amos stood up and spoke out for justice. This was equally true more than fifty years ago when an outsider named Martin Luther King Jr. stepped in front of a microphone on the steps of the Lincoln Memorial and included Amos's prophecy to confront comfortable peoples' complacency about America's lingering civil injustices and racial inequities.

"Let justice roll down like (mighty flood) waters," says the Lord. "And righteousness (cleansing and refreshing the nation) like an ever-flowing stream!"

For those who already feel comfortable, these words seem strange, even confrontational. Yet, for those who suffer injustice and disrespect, this image is one of the most beautiful in all of scripture.

A Prayer in Response

Eternal source of justice, pour down on my spirit like a mighty waterfall. I need to feel the weight of your will for me…to treat everyone fairly.

Eternal source of righteousness, cleanse my soul like a swift, ever-flowing stream. I need to feel the constant power of your will for me…to respect the dignity of every human being.

You have shown me how to be just in my dealings. You have shown me how to do right by others. So, draw me into the flow of your unquenchable desire for justice and righteousness that blesses your whole human family. *So be it!*

Friday

Amend your ways…
and let me dwell with you.

JEREMIAH 7:3

The prophet Jeremiah is called by God when he is a child. He has serious doubts and reasonable excuses—like us. "Ah, LORD God! Truly I do not know how to speak, for I am only a boy."

God is not persuaded in the least. "Do not say, 'I am only a boy' for you shall go where I send you and speak what I tell you. Do not be afraid, for I am with you" (Jeremiah 1:7-8, paraphrased).

From that day forward, Jeremiah is called upon to speak hard truths to the people of his nation (Judah) and Jerusalem. He struggles with his people—and also with his God. Jeremiah has much to say about the Lord's punishments for disobedience, but he also highlights the rewards of righteousness.

Through it all, Jeremiah repeats God's persistent desire (seven times in the first thirty-two chapters of this book).

Our Lord's desire is this: "You shall be my people, and I will be your God." This simple and profound hope should clarify everything we need to know about how to worship.

The good news that undergirds the prophecy of Jeremiah (and all the other prophets) is that God wants nothing more or less than to have a healthy, honest, and fruitful relationship with human partners who are willing to trust God's wisdom and—therefore—follow in God's ways.

"You shall be my people, and I will be your God," says the Lord through Jeremiah's prophecy to the Jewish people. Hundreds of years later, a Jewish Pharisee named Paul stands before the most intelligent, religious people of Athens and explains how God's promise is actually intended for all people. Indeed, Paul explains, God's desire is not just to live *with us* but to live *within us*. As with Abraham, God dreams of a world in which God's faithfulness gets expressed through us.

Saint Paul says: "The God who made the world and everything in it, who is Lord of heaven and earth, does not live in shrines made by human hands…this God set forth through one faithful person (Abraham) all the peoples and nations of the earth so that they would search, grope, and be able to find the Lord of heaven and earth. Indeed, this God is not far from any one of us. For it is in God that we live and move and have our being." (Find the unabridged speech I have lightly paraphrased in Acts 17:22-31.)

The good news, according to Jeremiah, is that God desires to dwell with us. That's not all. We learned on the second day of Lent that God's own Spirit is planted within us. So, what the Lord is really asking through Jeremiah is for us to amend our lives so that God's life and blessing will more clearly shine through us.

A Prayer in Response

In you, O God, I live and move and have my being. And I believe that you, likewise, want to live and move within me. I want to amend my life so that I may be a worthy temple for your Holy Spirit, and so that your faithfulness will shine through me as a blessing for others. *So be it!*

Saturday

Do not heap up empty phrases.

MATTHEW 6:7

Jesus, the Word of God, knows all about the power of words and phrases. Words contain the power to create light and life, a world of incredible variety and vitality. Words also contain the power to destroy life, relationships, and so much else. Many of the words of wisdom contained in the book of Proverbs urge caution about the power of words.

Jesus knows that while words and phrases contain power that can be wielded for good or for ill, they can also be empty of such power. Sometimes words and phrases are simply vacuous sounds, shallow arrangements of letters that lack authenticity or meaningfulness.

When Jesus preaches his Sermon on the Mount (Matthew chapters 5-7), he wants us to know that he—the Word of God—recognizes the difference. "Do not waste your time heaping up empty phrases when you pray," he says. They are not valuable and—therefore—not valued. Our Lord is only interested in words that contain the power of truth, meaning, and purpose.

Thoughtless prayers of adoration are just empty flattery. Prayers of thanksgiving, which are not heartfelt, sound like pabulum to God's ears. Prayers of confession without any authentic desire to change are wisps of air. Rote intercessions and petitions devoid of any true willingness to participate in God's response sound like a noisy gong or a clanging cymbal. (See 1 Corinthians 13 for Saint Paul's powerful message about the meaninglessness of empty words that lack the power of love.)

This week, we have learned how God prefers to be worshiped and respected. The common thread of all these reflections is that our actions speak louder than words. Therefore, we should make sure that the speech we use in our verbal prayers is brimful of honest intention to act for the glory of God and the blessing of other people.

A Prayer in Response

Dear Jesus, you are the Word by which all other words are measured. Fill my heart with such love for you that my words and phrases are filled with sincerity and truth.

I want to pray like I mean it. I want to worship and adore you with a thankful heart. I want my confessions to convey deep sorrow and humble repentance. I want to intercede for my neighbors in thought, word, and deed.

Your Spirit, mingled with my spirit, will produce authentic prayers and fruitful actions that glorify your name and magnify your merciful love for the world. *So be it!*

The Honest Truth

Authentic Worship Means...

Blessing Others

Opening Our Hearts for Healing

Offering Our First, Best Fruits

Doing the Right Thing Seven Days a Week

Letting Justice Roll Down Like Water

Amending Our Broken Ways

For GOODNESS' Sake

The week when God's actions speak even more loudly than words.

Holy Week

The Sunday of the Passion: Palm Sunday

Jesus chooses humility.

You will find a donkey...and a colt with her;
untie them and bring them to me.

MATTHEW 21:2

Staging a triumphant entrance into the capital city on the most important holiday weekend of the year is not something your average king would leave to chance. Every detail would be carefully planned and precisely orchestrated so that even an average king would look dignified and powerful, riding in the shiniest gold chariot and being pulled by the largest stallions.

It's obvious that our king—Jesus—is far below average. And he has chosen his status on purpose. Jesus does not even own a donkey that he can ride. He must send two disciples to look for a donkey and a colt that he can borrow for a couple of hours. We feel the anxiety of those disciples who are tasked with untying someone else's animals when Jesus says, "If anyone says anything to you, just say this, 'The Lord needs them.'" Imagine that! Imagine the Lord, the Almighty, needing anything.

The most important week in the earthly life of Jesus unfolds like a master class in humility. He begins just as the prophet, Zechariah, had foretold: "Look, your king is coming to you, humble and mounted on a donkey, and on a colt, the foal of a donkey."[1] And it continues downhill from there.

After borrowing donkeys for the parade, Jesus must borrow a room for his last supper with the disciples. Ultimately, we know that his dead body will be buried in a borrowed tomb. Jesus wants to erase any doubt in anyone's mind that he is up above it all. Just the opposite—Jesus is down in it all… with us.

On the Saturday of the fourth week of Lent, we heard Jesus state his life's purpose: "The Son of Man came not to be served, but to serve." Finally, we have arrived at the final week—our Holy Week—when Christ's actions are speaking even more loudly than these words.

---

1 Zechariah 9:9

A Prayer in Response

King of all creation, why did you insist that your disciples not look up to you or be afraid of you? Even in the hour of your earthly triumph, your most devoted followers looked down on you, seated upon a borrowed colt, the foal of a donkey.

Thank you for choosing to be with us at all times and in all places, especially down in the trenches when life gets hard or scary. We need a savior who can relate to us in our weakness.

Your willingness to be compassionate and to suffer with us is the very reason we will exalt you above all other kings, forever. *So be it!*

Monday of Holy Week

Jesus overturns the barriers to God's grace.

My house shall be called a house of prayer; but you are making it a den of robbers.

MATTHEW 21:13

When Jesus was just thirty-one days old, his parents followed the law. They brought him to the temple in Jerusalem to present their firstborn son to the Lord. Since they could not afford the price of a sacrificial lamb, they purchased a pair of turtle doves instead. As we learned last Tuesday, the law included this merciful exception for poor people.

In that sacrificial-based worship environment, vendors sold animals and birds for the people to bring to the priests as offerings for God. And since graven images were prohibited by Jewish law, money changers helped keep Caesar's image (on Roman coins) from showing up in the temple treasury.

We don't know all the details of the day an adult Jesus disrupts this essential commercial enterprise. Indeed, while Matthew, Mark, and Luke pinpoint the story during the last week of Jesus's earthly life, John's Gospel describes it as happening years earlier. (Perhaps Jesus got angry at them more than once?!)

What we do know is that Jesus is absolutely passionate about his Father's unconditional love and mercy for every living soul. He envisions the temple as the prophet Isaiah had described it: "a house of prayer for all people" (56:7).

Yet, the reality was starkly different. The money changers, animal vendors, and priests were literally standing in the way of God's grace. Jesus's passionate, righteous anger flares, and he physically overturns their profitable barrier.

Jesus then borrows from the words of the prophet Jeremiah, who denounced those who oppressed poor widows, orphans, and immigrants and pretended as if the temple belonged to them. Jesus repeats this searing truth out loud: "You are making my Father's House into a den of robbers."

This past Friday, we heard the positive side of Jeremiah's prophecy about God's desire to dwell with—and within—us. On this Monday of Holy Week, Jesus shares the challenging side of Jeremiah's prophecy. God rejects hypocrisy, especially when it stands in the way of grace and mercy.

A Prayer in Response

THANK YOU, Jesus, for standing up for the poor and speaking out against greed and hypocrisy. Help me to remember that the opposite of love is not anger but indifference. Give me strength and courage to stand up and speak out with you. And grant me humility and meekness to avoid standing in the way of our heavenly Father's unconditional love and mercy. *So be it!*

Tuesday of Holy Week

Jesus scolds the arrogant.

All who exalt themselves will be humbled,
and all who humble themselves will be exalted.

Matthew 23:12

The Gospel according to Matthew records a long, intractable debate between Jesus and the top leaders of Judah—the chief priests, Sadducees, scribes, and Pharisees. These influential, religious men stand in perfect solidarity with all the political, strong men (the Herodians and the Romans).

Opposite them—literally and figuratively—stands Jesus, the Galilean who eats and drinks with disreputable people. Except for a few daring disciples, this outsider is all alone. This wandering rabbi, who is preoccupied with the needs of the poor, the sick, the hungry, and the dying, stands alone.

Jesus and those religious men share a common theology about obedience to God. So, Jesus connects this shared idea of obedience to God with a practical theology of what it looks like in real life to love your neighbor as yourself.

These exalted men know the holiness code of Leviticus better than anyone. Yet, their failure to refrain from slander, greed, or grudge-bearing is obvious. Their failure to speak against the injustices of Roman oppression of their poor, neglected Jewish neighbors is breathtaking.

Simply put, the religious leaders love the wealth and prestige of their power-sharing arrangement with the political leaders. They do not love their neighbors as much as themselves.

Standing in front of these men who are dressed in soft robes with pockets full of Roman coins and hearts full of malice, Jesus harshly scolds them. They know they must silence him by killing him. According to John's Gospel, this is the fifth time the religious leaders have either plotted or attempted to murder Jesus (Chapters 7, 8, 10, and 11). This time, they will succeed.

Jesus does not have to die because God needs an atoning sacrifice for human sin. (We have thoroughly reviewed the Lord's disdain for sacrificial appeasement.) Jesus dies because he stands up and speaks out against the injustices perpetrated by the very people who are most responsible for ensuring God's justice for God's people. Jesus is murdered because he refuses to be silent.

A Prayer in Response

DEAR JESUS, you were willing to scold the religious and political men who had the power to kill you. They took your life because they refused to follow your teaching. Thank you for standing up to their arrogance and for showing us a different kind of life, a humble life, loving God wholeheartedly and loving your neighbors as much as yourself. And so, I exalt you, O Lord, now and forever! *So be it!*

Wednesday of Holy Week

Jesus defends a generous woman.

Let her alone.

Mark 14:6

Jesus is consistent when it comes to taking sides with women. Whenever the gospels record a story of a woman being persecuted, questioned, dismissed, or ignored, Jesus generally has something to say about it, and it tends to be one-sided. He even stands up for a woman caught in the act of adultery—a capital crime in first-century Judah—and chooses instead to accost the innocent men who want to hold her accountable!

In the middle of his last week of earthly life, Jesus is in Bethany, a short and safe distance from Jerusalem. He is taking a break from his intense struggles with the powerful religious leaders at the temple. As Jesus sits down for a meal with friends, a woman walks up with an expensive alabaster jar filled with very costly ointment.

When she breaks the fancy jar and pours all the contents upon Jesus's head, it is not a subtle act of kindness. No! Her behavior is absolutely over the top. In this startling moment, she becomes a sort of prodigal daughter, acting recklessly and extravagantly.

The righteous indignation is swift, "What a waste! Why wasn't the ointment sold for a lot of money to be given to the poor?" This harsh criticism does not arise from the usually judgmental Pharisees. Rather, these complaints are spoken by Jesus's own friends and disciples. Jesus doesn't care. His defense of this generous woman is unambiguous: "Let her alone!" he demands.

Jesus applauds this prodigal daughter who demonstrates her recklessly extravagant love and devotion to him. In two days' time, we will look up at a Roman cross and see the Son of God demonstrate recklessly extravagant love and devotion for us.

There will always be those who cluck their tongues and say, "Such a waste!" What Jesus wants us to see is that extravagant loving-kindness is a good thing, and we are all capable of showing it.

When Jesus says, "You always have the poor with you," he is not dismissing their legitimate needs. Rather, he is challenging us to act like this prodigal daughter—and like him—showing extravagant loving-kindness without holding back.

A Prayer in Response

Dear Jesus, you exalted the prodigal daughter when your friends criticized her reckless extravagance. Two days later, you gave us the ultimate example of prodigal loving-kindness. Help me to be as swift and generous in my love for you and in my devotion to the poor whom you consider beloved as well. *So be it!*

Maundy Thursday

Jesus washes dirty feet.

Do you know what I have done to you?

JOHN 13:12

It is completely backward for a master to kneel at the feet of his servants or for a teacher to bow down to his students. Yet, this is precisely how Jesus spends his last supper with the disciples. Jesus gets down on his knees and washes the dirty feet of his friends. The teacher is still teaching—by example—how to love and serve undeserving people.

Through this simple but profound act of service, Jesus shows how much he loves his disciples, loving them to the end. His miraculous love extends to his betrayer, his triple-denier, and the rest of the disciples who will desert him. Jesus loves all of them—every last one of his disappointing followers. (This is really good news for the rest of us disappointing followers of Jesus.)

For several years, this small group of disciples has followed Jesus everywhere. Through various stages of belief and disbelief, they have watched Jesus feed the hungry and heal the sick. They've seen Jesus restore sight to the blind, hearing to the deaf, sanity to the mentally ill, and mobility to the paralytics. These disciples have even witnessed Jesus bring the dead back to life.

Jesus has done these things for their family members and for total strangers. Jesus has performed miracles for good Jewish folks and for occupying, enemy soldiers. He's helped respectable leaders and nasty, belligerent outcasts. In all his travels, far and wide, Jesus never seems to have met a single person whom he considered undeserving of God's loving-kindness.

When you have a leader who is that amazing, you look up to him!

At their last supper together, Jesus knows that his disciples need another perspective. They need an opportunity not only to look up to him but also to look down on him. We, disciples, need to look down and see our Lord kneeling like a slave to wash the dirty feet of undeserving people.

It is easy to exalt Jesus for all his miraculous achievements. Yet, we must also not lose sight of his humble service. At the last supper, we plainly see that Jesus meant exactly what he said about himself, "The Son of Man came not to be served, but to serve" (Matthew 20:28).

"Do you know what I have done?" Jesus asks. We may be as speechless as the first disciples, but we do know what our Lord has done. He has shown us how to love and serve like him.

A Prayer in Response

Dear Jesus, it is easy to look up to you for all the extraordinary things you've done. I know I must also look down on you if I am to be moved to follow your humble example. I need your help if I am to love and serve people, even those who might betray and deny me. *So be it!*

Good Friday

Jesus forgives his torturers.

Father, forgive them!

Luke 23:34

The miracle of God's atonement actually begins before Jesus dies.

If we believe God when God says, "I desire mercy, not sacrifice," then we are able to see the miracle of atonement already happening when Jesus offers divine mercy to his torturers...*while* he is being tortured.

We can trust the words of God the Father, who says, "I desire steadfast love and not sacrifice" (Hosea 6:6). And we can trust those same words when they are repeated by God the Son, who says, "Learn what this means (about my Father): 'I desire mercy, not sacrifice'" (Matthew 9:13).

Good Friday is the day we learn the full extent of what God means. Hanging on a Roman cross, bleeding and dying, Jesus shows steadfast love and mercy, even to his torturers.

This extraordinary moment reveals God's unshakeable desire for reconciliation with the world God so loves.

We first encounter the quintessential Old Testament definition of God's character on the second Friday of Lent with these words: "I am merciful and gracious, slow to anger, and abounding in steadfast love and faithfulness, keeping steadfast love for the thousandth generation, forgiving iniquity and transgression and sin..." On Good Friday, Jesus offers clear, living proof of this character before he dies. Like Father, like Son.

In the first chapter of the Gospel according to Saint John, he first states the obvious, "No one has ever seen God." True enough. Then, John sets us up to see and hear all the ways Jesus will reveal the fullness of the Lord when he writes, "It is God the only Son, who is close to the Father's heart, who has made Him known" (John 1:18).

Jesus makes the glorious character of God knowable—seeable, hearable, touchable, and even tastable. He does this repeatedly, but never more clearly than the miraculous moment on Good Friday when he forgives the absolute worst evil that humankind could possibly do—willful torture and murder. If God can reconcile that, God can reconcile anything. If God can forgive those who put Jesus to death, God can forgive any trespass and forgive any debt.

Before Jesus offers the perfect sacrifice of all time, he offers the perfect forgiveness of all time, for all people. He does so when he pleads, "Father, forgive them."

A Prayer in Response

FORGIVING GOD, you showed the depth of your mercy in the face of the worst evil and hatred. Even then, you revealed steadfast love and forgiveness. I am forever thankful for your mercy. I am forever inspired to share it, trusting that steadfast love and mercy is what you also desire from me. *So be it!*

Holy Saturday

Jesus endures the sting of death.

silence

LUKE 23:50-53

This is the day we hear the full depth of God's love in God's first language—silence.

Today, we experience the full lengths Jesus is willing to go in order to live and die as one of us.

Notice where we are—at a tomb in a garden.

On Thursday night, Jesus was in another garden, the Garden of Gethsemane. *Gethsemane* in Hebrew means crushing place. It was the place just outside Jerusalem where olives were pressed—crushed—to make oil. The name fits. It becomes the place where Jesus is hard-pressed—even crushed—by the burden that lies before him and by the abandonment of his friends around him.

Think back to the very beginning of Lent. Our story begins in a garden—a garden filled with life and goodness, where

God dreams of an honest, fruitful, just, and peaceful partnership with humans. Instead, we choose deception, greed, blame, and, ultimately, violence.

Today, we stand in a garden of death and sadness. It appears the story has reached its logical conclusion. Predictably, humans have once again rejected the dream of God—this time by violently rejecting the Son of God.

Death is real, even for God.

And there is nothing we can do about that except honor this sacrifice by God for us.

There are no words that can adequately express the honor and glory due to our God in light of this immeasurable gift.

Today, we honor the full depth of God's love using God's first language—silence.

A Prayer in Response

Most holy and loving God,

(*Silence*—for a period that feels reverent and sacrificial… five minutes, thirty minutes, an hour, or all day. You have the freedom to decide.)

So be it!

Jesus rises from the dead!

Peace be with you.

JOHN 20:19

When Jesus first appears to Mary Magdalene and then to his other disciples, he says, "*Shalom*—peace be with you." I suspect he is trying to allay their fears, for they are still confused and frightened. Yet, his greeting also expresses a whole lot more than just "calm down!"

Jesus is describing the full goodness and beauty of life as intended by God in the very beginning—honest, fruitful, just, and peaceful partnership with God and with our neighbors. The earliest disciples get to taste the first fruits of eternal life even before they die. And this changes everything!

The peace of the Lord leads them to say and do things they were previously afraid to say and do. The peace of the Lord emboldens them to heal and restore people who are sick and broken. The peace of the Lord inspires them to share literally everything they own with one another.

The peace of the Lord propels them out from Jerusalem into all the world. The peace of the Lord expands their ability and willingness to see the true goodness in people, foods, and customs that were previously considered against the Law, unclean, or off limits.

Maybe we should ask ourselves this question: "If Jesus Christ actually has conquered death and proven that God's life and love are victorious over everything, what are we waiting for?"

The peace of the Lord really does have the power to change everything, just as it did on Easter Day when Jesus first announces it. This peace utterly transforms individuals and communities. And whenever people are willing to claim it and share it, this peace multiplies like loaves and fishes.

Shalom—the peace of the Lord—is a gift that goes back to the very beginning in creation. *Shalom*—the peace of the Lord—is reconfirmed in the glorious rainbow after the flood. *Shalom*—the peace of the Lord —is offered repeatedly by our God of steadfast love and mercy throughout the everlasting covenant story of the Old Testament.

And then, *Shalom*—the peace of the Lord—strikes like lightning on that first Easter Day when death is swallowed up in the victory of Jesus Christ, who makes the whole creation new again!

A Prayer in Response

RISEN LORD, you overcame death in order to share the gift of peace with us—fullness of life forever more. Why do I hesitate to trust your gift? Why am I reluctant to embrace the power of your life and love?

Inspire me to live in the power of your resurrection! Make me an instrument of your peace! Give me a confident voice to proclaim the Good News of your resurrection when I say, "The peace of the Lord be always with you!" *So be it!*

The Honest Truth

Jesus...

Chooses Humility

Overturns Barriers

Rejects Arrogance

Favors Generosity

Serves | Forgives

Is Willing to Die | Lives

For Goodness' Sake

Another Easter Story

Jesus is with us, even when we cannot see.

Oh, how foolish you are,
and how slow of heart to believe...

LUKE 24:25

On the road to Emmaus, Jesus has a little fun at his disciples' expense. When Cleopas and his friend are talking about all the terrible things that happened to Jesus in Jerusalem, he has the chutzpah to ask them, "What things?" as if he does not know...as if he is not the one to whom they happened. It is a mischievous way to start a conversation.

What does Jesus do first? He opens their eyes to the scriptures (the Old Testament) in order to help them see how the God who is gracious and merciful, slow to anger and of great kindness, and abounding in steadfast love—this God—will stop at nothing to give us the fruitful, peaceful life intended for us from the beginning.

And stopping at nothing, we try to destroy this promise by torturing and murdering the Son of God. Our Lord even forgives that.

And this is how love wins out over hate! This is how life conquers death!

Those disciples still do not understand. They still do not recognize him. To their credit, they invite Jesus to join them for dinner anyway. And he is revealed to them in the breaking of the bread.

I wrote this book to serve a similar purpose: to offer a fresh, new look at the Old Testament scriptures and to have a conversation with our Lord on the road of Lent. If you are like me, you still have questions. You still have doubts. We wonder how all this could be.

We should take a cue from these two disciples who meet Jesus without knowing it. We should open our minds, our hearts, and our homes to welcome the love of God more closely into our lives. Maybe like them, when we least expect it, our eyes will be opened.

I believe with all my heart that this is God's desire and delight for the whole human family. So, may the peace of the Lord be always with you!

A Prayer in Response

RISEN LORD, be known to us in the breaking of the bread… and in all the other unexpected ways that your grace and mercy enter our lives. I can be as foolish and slow of heart as the disciples who walked with you to Emmaus. I admit it. I need your victorious love to sustain me. I need your victorious life to give me peace. *So be it!*

Epilogue

Oh yes, you did laugh.

GENESIS 18:15

I hope you have enjoyed discovering the depth and breadth of God's honest words through the stories, songs, and prophecies of old. I hope some of these quotations helped you reflect upon God's character more broadly and deeply. I hope some of these prayers encouraged you to respond to God more honestly and directly. Finally, I hope some of these words made you laugh.

This reminds me of another story I simply cannot resist sharing because it reveals an important aspect of our life with God.

A messenger from God tells old Abraham something preposterous—that he and Sarah, despite their advanced age, will have a son. Sarah is eavesdropping on this conversation from inside the tent and laughs to herself.

"After I have grown old, and my husband is old, shall I have pleasure?" she quite reasonably asks.

The Lord asks Abraham, "Why did Sarah laugh? Is anything too wonderful for (me) to do?"

Sarah denies having laughed because she is afraid of God. "I did not laugh," she lies.

God knows better! "Oh yes, you did laugh!" says the Lord.

Thousands of years later, there is still a lot about God that is hard to believe. We are quite reasonable to question, doubt, and even laugh at some of these things.

I think the biblical message is clear. It is okay to react as a "normal" person would. Just be honest about it!

God's honest words are intended to challenge, comfort, and inspire us to collaborate as human partners for goodness' sake. Honest to goodness is the direction in which God is moving, and we are always invited to travel along. It's the journey through which we are able to discover the truth and beauty of loving God.

The bottom line is that God is love. And love is always honest. As Saint Paul wrote to the Corinthians, "Love rejoices in the truth." For this reason, we can trust Love—we can trust *God*—to "bear all things, believe all things, hope all things, and endure all things…love never ends" (1 Corinthians 13:6-8).

This is the essence of the Good News, which has been revealed repeatedly through the words and deeds of God found in the Old Testament, the words and deeds of Jesus recorded in the New Testament, and above all, in the miracle of Easter, which still makes us want to laugh, sing, and dance with joy.

The Good News, simply put, is that Love never ends!

Thanks be to God. *So be it!*

About the Author

Furman Buchanan is an Episcopal priest and author with two decades of experience helping people discover the truth and beauty of a loving God. He is known for teaching and preaching that is accessible and relatable, even for those who lack much knowledge of the Bible.

Buchanan attributes the vitality of the three congregations he has served to the deep hunger that faithful people naturally have for experiencing and sharing the goodness of God's love. *Honest to Goodness* was borne out of a desire to help people see the vivid connection between the Father, Son, and Holy Spirit—one loving God who calls upon beloved people to share what they have received.

He and his wife, Kim, live in Mt. Pleasant, South Carolina, where he serves as the rector of historic Christ Episcopal Church. They have three adult daughters.

Also available by Furman Buchanan: *The Gifts of God for the People of God: Exploring Worship in the Episcopal Church*, winner of the Illumination Book Awards silver medal for theology.

About Forward Movement

Forward Movement inspires disciples and empowers evangelists. We live out our call as a discipleship ministry by publishing daily reflections and online resources. People around the world read daily devotions through *Forward Day by Day*, which is also available in Spanish (*Adelante Día a Día*) and Braille, online, as a podcast, and as an app for your smartphone.

A ministry of the Episcopal Church since 1935, Forward Movement is a nonprofit organization funded by sales of resources and gifts from generous donors.

Learn more about Forward Movement and our work, at forwardmovement.org or venadelante.org.